Soul Diving
from My
Giant's Eyebrow

Soul Diving
from My
Giant's Eyebrow

AN INSPIRATIONAL JOURNEY TO
ACHIEVING INTUITIVENESS

Maria Garay Reynolds

Archway Publishing books may be ordered through booksellers or by contacting:

Archway Publishing
1663 Liberty Drive
Bloomington, IN 47403
www.archwaypublishing.com
1-(888)-242-5904

ISBN: 978-1-4808-0372-5 (sc)
ISBN: 978-1-4808-0374-9 (hc)
ISBN: 978-1-4808-0373-2 (e)

Library of Congress Control Number: 2013920966

Printed in the United States of America

Archway Publishing rev. date: 11/20/13

I dedicate this book to my friend Joann Duham and Rev. Jeffrey Serkin. The day I walked into their lives, I was in divine hands that changed my life and the lives of many others.

Acknowledgments

I made a trip to my mother's grave, which I had not visited since she transitioned because I could not make myself go to her grave site. Her persistence and our conversation at that time is how I gave birth to this book.

Before I heard her voice telling me I must come and visit. Night after night in my dreams and day after day in my meditations I would hear her.

Mama gave me the gift of old memories that allowed me to heal on a level deep in my soul. But even with all the work I had done, there were still unrecognized resentments hiding. I am grateful to learn how deep resentments and ignorance of why and how our feelings can cause sudden and unexplained illnesses and poor choices that do not work out.

This whole book took place at my mama's grave site and at the bank of the Sacramento River where my giant took form.

Preface

Everything starts with the consciousness that conflict is an unavoidable part of our lives, although we may find our beliefs are in powerful contrast to our feelings. When we truly know who we are, we unveil that we are one with all life, without separation. Every facet of life on earth is interconnected to a network that bonds us to our true selves.

The word *God* comes with the baggage of historical time—of churches and contention and fear. In this book I convey the idea that we are all energetic beings from an intelligent, spiritual source of energy that is present and that radiates throughout our universe. It creates all life from one source, which is God or what a person calls God.

Energy is a clumsy word. It does not denote how alive the body is—how trillions of cells can cooperate to create a whole. Our soul is pure energy light, that translates into endless energy (intuition) that guides you on your path. We are each a spiritual being experiencing a physical body on our remarkable planet.

I am intelligence. I am life. I am truth. I am love. I am Spirit. I am the source that is us. The name *om*, the name of the source, is what the ancient people of Asia used to repeat over and over and repeat even now when they meditate. They hold their breath while speaking it. As they chant, it means "Good beyond Good." It is part of understanding and believing in the following components:

◊ I am *omnipresent*—the fact of being present, existing everywhere at the same time. This, in turn, becomes the awareness of the energy in your own body at all times.
◊ I am *omnipotent*, having unlimited or absolute power or authority, such as the power that humans have to live our lives as we choose.
◊ I am *omniscient*, knowing everything. The universe is a gift to us from the day we are each born.

This is what I found on my life journey with my angels, my guides, and my mama's help.

Everything that happens to us is a gift for growth that reminds us to look within our souls to the omnipresence of who we are. The more difficult the experiences we suffer in our daily lives, the greater the gifts from the universe for a healing process that teaches us how to exist in the present moment. When you learn to tune in and listen to your intuition—your soul's voice—you understand that your wisdom originated with you at the time of your birth. In order to give or receive healing, you must know without a doubt that you are part of everything—a spiritual being in a human body.

This book explains, in simple terms, how to listen and do your own soul diving to see how you are intuitive and all-knowing. Gut feelings earn their name from the place in the body where they make themselves known—a pang in your gut when you are doing something wrong or a butterfly zing when your body approves. Learning to use your intuition will guide you when logic fails. Psychic ability is made up of truth, love, substance, and your own intelligence.

The omnipresent, omnipotent, and omniscient being of who we are combines the wonder and truth of receiving information in its many forms.

Spiritual thinking is the pioneer that opens the way to new birth, but it must be followed by spiritual actions. The universe is made up of all existing things, including the earth with all its creatures, the heavens, and the galaxies. However, the physical manifestation of man and woman is the highest expression of the source of life. To know your own self is to know the source of life—the wholeness of the universe.

From the time we are infants, we develop the habit of thought that makes us believe we cannot be all things. This habit makes us believe we will not break the cycle that tells us we cannot know all, and that we, as humans, are not source in action. That cycle of believing in our limitations needs to be broken to allow us to recognize that we can see all, hear all, heal, and truly know. Only by understanding that humans are perfect and have no limitations to their abilities can we realize we are omnipotent.

When you do not listen to that gut feeling, dreams show you how to find meaning in your life. American Indians believe that the Great Spirit offered dreams to guide and inspire the soul.

Edgar Cayce, the great American psychic, once declared, "Visions and dreams are given for the benefit of the individual growth."

Dreams are the most frequent place you first receive information that tells you the subconscious is talking to you. The conscious mind is still during sleep, allowing the true self to hear clues and problem-solve solutions. Train yourself to see those red flags go up, and your gut feeling becomes alive with information for your waking life.

In the following chapters, I write about my own soul-diving experiences that started around the age of five and my subsequent adventures retrieving my memory of how and when I first altered myself. At that young age, I found it necessary to change myself in order to be accepted. I had to experience all that hurt in order to heal completely and become my true self.

CHAPTER 1

My experiences and knowledge with intuition started one step at time. Intuition is a part of our nature and coded in our DNA. All life is connected with the same DNA; therefore, we are all from one source. To know this is true freedom. How we process that knowledge produces and controls all phenomena in our material world. Spiritual knowledge is still in the primitive state of an individual's fundamental character or disposition.

A small part of our intuition is character and disposition. Intuition is not a gift until it is developed as the stronger feature of being in touch with our senses. Some, but not all, humans enjoy this state of being. Intuition has many facets and shows up in many ways, but it always hits that gut feeling of knowing that something is about to happen.

Everything that happens on any given day and the choices we make within that day all make up a gift for growth—that includes smells, sounds, feelings, colors, animals, nature that help us to be a collective whole.

Listening is also part of intuition. It can become an art of awareness. It is paying attention to the details of sounds for the information that they can impart—from the sound of the smallest insect to the noisiest city. An example is the sound of your breath, heart, or pulse. All are information on your health. Frequencies are a constant source of energy that can be heard like an invisible telephone or like telegraph messages. Thoughts generated from this earth and the universe give information that can be tapped by listening more carefully.

I learned to listen to my physical and metaphysical senses, which are all related. Learning to use one of our senses can lead to using others. I started teaching my children how to listen at an early age. I would take them out during the day to a quiet place. I would have them close their eyes and tell me all the sounds they heard. Then I would take them out at night to listen to sounds of the dark and interpret the harmony of insects singing. When we pay attention, we can hear the rhythm of the world between all life forms. All life forms speak in different ways. Just listen, and you will hear them.

Rhythm is not only sound but a natural movement of life. Listen and tune into rhythms that allow your energy to flow, and your gut will tell you what intuition is speaking.

Taking your cue from all the sounds and memories you have gathered helps create a *bridge of wholeness* to find your psychic ability. The bridge is remembering who we are from the time of birth. When we are young, we are pure energy beings living in the moment; nothing else exists. We are super beings as children playing, flying, and becoming anyone and anything we wish to be. As children, we do not care about the surrounding world, because doubt is not a part of the day. Perfection in that moment is the secret bridge to intuition.

I can now remember my wholeness and the answers I held within myself. Smells are also a large portion of the information I receive on a regular basis. All living matter and humans have an individual fragrance. A fragrance can give you a lot of information, and it can bring up memories.

I visited the mighty redwoods to touch and admire how ancient these trees are. I sat at the root close to the trunk and visually became part of the root system. I received visions and parts of myself in other lifetimes. I could see myself in another dimension. All of this happened at the same time. The earth under me was warm and loving.

When I had a nagging feeling and could not let it go, I would find out what it was telling me. I call this gut feeling being in the present moment. Tune in and become sensitive to the energy surrounding you. As energy beings, we can tune to a higher frequency, much like a radio, and hear our intuition sending out messages. Humans can learn to tune and refine their own frequencies.

Our atmosphere is filled with spiritual activity—the energy of other beings. Intuition, spirits, orbs, and ghosts occur on different planes with important differences. Spirits are ectoplasm and appear anywhere, and ghosts are imprints of life that is repeating itself, like a negative of a picture. Orbs are energy beings. This activity takes place behind the curtain of unawareness, which humans cannot see unless they work on being sensitive beings.

Studying and working with spiritual energy as helped me to understand, see, and hear spiritual activity that is always around me, day and night.

Intuition and psychic powers are related but are entirely different. Intuition is an inherited part of humans' and animals' survival instincts. As living beings, we experience daily doses of knowing when there is imminent danger or the low-level feeling that something is off. Gut feelings are always present whether we realize it or not. Learning to depend on and trust our intuition when our souls speak is profound and attainable.

My mama was intuitive, but it scared her. She did not know what it was, so she protected me and herself from what she thought were unknown evil forces with prayer. I wanted to tell my mama about intuition so she would not be afraid, but I was too young and did not have enough knowledge.

After her death, I went into mediation to call her and said, "Mama, this is what I would have said to you when you were alive: do not be afraid of intuition."

CHAPTER 2

Journey to the Bear Funeral

*F*rom a sound sleep, I heard what sounded like a phone ringing. It was muffled and far away, so I just rolled over and did not pay attention to it. The sound got closer and closer until it completely woke me. I realized that it was my phone, and my heart skipped a beat. I could hear myself saying, "Oh no," when I jumped to pick the phone up. When I raised the phone to my ear, I heard my friend Cheryl's voice on the line. I said, "Hello, are you all right? What is going on?"

Her voice was sad and raspy as she told me that her father had passed away. I did not know what to say except that I was on my way. Cheryl has been my best friend since we met at my workplace, Sacramento Municipal Court. Robert my husband and I helped her parents with their property in Dunlap, California. Through the years, they have all become our family. We packed up the motor home and headed for Sacramento, California, in October 2010.

The service was both touching and difficult, but it was important to be standing next to my friend. During the ceremony, thoughts of my mother flooded my whole being. In an instant, I knew that Murphy, Cheryl's father, had somehow talked to my mama. He relayed the message that would bring my mother and me together. What a great gift from Murphy.

I told my husband, Robert, that I had to go find my mother's gravesite and visit her because I clearly heard Murphy's voice telling me, "Your mother is waiting for you." After the service, the entire group went to a restaurant for our last gathering. This was to support each other on this painful day, but also to celebrate Murphy's life.

Robert and I went back to Cal Expo, where our motor home was parked, to rest and take care of our dogs. After dinner, we talked about going to find my mother and heading out early for Woodland, California.

I woke up early and could hear Mama calling that she was waiting for me. We put the dogs in the car and started our journey. Little did I know how much my life would change.

After forty-seven years, I was on my way to find the cemetery. We had to pass by Elkhorn Ferry, where I was raised, so memories quickly emerged. I'll keep those to myself for now. We found the cemetery, drove through the last gate, and found a place to park.

It felt strange standing in the middle of the cemetery, bracing myself against the cold, howling wind. The autumn leaves danced and whipped dust all around me. I started shivering and let out a deep sigh, pulling tightly on my scarf. I struggled to wrap it around my ears and across my nose to keep the wind from stinging my face. It also kept the pungent smell of wet leaves and decomposing grass clippings from assaulting my nostrils.

I stopped for a moment in the middle of three old, tall grave stones, admiring the workmanship and wondering how much the three people were loved. At the same time, I gazed at fluffy clouds as they covered the sun. The wind was still pushing the clouds fast. Between the moving clouds, the sun felt warm on my face. I took a deep breath through my nose, letting the air move out though my open lips while I searched rows of graves hoping to recognize my mother's plot after so many years.

I began whispering under my breath, telling my mama, "Show me where you are buried. After all, you are the one who called me here."

My intuition and the sound of her voice kept pushing me, like enormous hands, to find her. Then it felt as if she grabbed my hand and pulled me. I always act on my intuition, but this was something I had not experienced before.

As a child, I never gave a serious thought to who my mama was except how awful she was when she embarrassed me. I was so busy in my own world; I was blind to who she was as a woman with her own problems. She was just my mama, and today I needed her.

I continued along the narrow path without success. My shoes were wet and heavy with mud, and I was fighting back tears of frustration. To make it worse, the wind was blowing even harder. I yelled out, "Where are you?" I stood still for a moment and held my breath, waiting to hear a response or feel a hunch.

A sense of desperation set in as I looked for help, but the grounds office was closed. Walking at a fast pace toward my car, I started to justify leaving the grounds without seeing her. Finally, I cried out loud, "I am here," and threw my arms up in frustration. I slowed my walk in hopes of finding her before I reached the car. I could not shake the emotional feeling of why I had to find her. I opened the car door and took one last look. With a big sigh, I closed the door and said, "Well, that was that."

Driving away I turned to my husband. "I did what was asked of me. I came, and that is enough." Robert put his hand over mine, assuring me we would return and find her.

I responded, "Yes, maybe we can find the caretaker and ask, but right at this minute, I am not in the mood to come back." We got into the warm car, and my chilled bones were starting to heat up as we left the cemetery. I could hear my dogs and Robert in the background through the noise of the traffic. Closing my eyes to relax, I began reminiscing about my high school days.

Driving back through downtown Woodland, I noticed that it had not changed much after all these years. I pointed out to Robert the street my high school was on, and that period of time started to move back into my thoughts. I could hear my heart beating faster, and my chest felt heavy with excitement and sadness.

Adjusting the vent to direct more heat on me, I enjoyed the warm sun shining through the windshield. Out of nowhere, old memories of my high school days popped into my head. The old feeling of being back in school came rushing in, filling my gut with wrenching pain and loneliness. I raised my hands across my chest and embraced myself in a hug as my body cringed.

High school had been a lonely, hard place for me. I cried and howled from a place deep in my soul because I felt hated. At the time, I thought it might be because of the way I looked, dressed, talked, or acted. I wanted to be liked and accepted.

One of my biggest frustrations was that I did not have anyone to talk to, not only about being psychic, but also about clothes, manners, and other things young girls should know. I could not understand why I was not liked. I asked myself many times, "What is wrong with me?" I wanted to run and hide on my "giant" as I have so many times. There were many days I would stand at my locker sobbing so deeply that there was no air, just gasps. As students passed by me, pointing and laughing, I wanted to disappear. I could not stop the tears from running down my face into my mouth. To this day, I can still remember those salty tears.

I quickly moved out of those old feelings by replacing them with wonderful memories of my mother. I also gave thanks for lessons learned and felt surprised the past had popped up. I spoke softly to Robert. "I am so glad my high school days are long gone."

I relaxed back into the warm, moving car, closing my eyes and enjoying the rhythm and the vibration of the road. After a few minutes, I was somewhere between awake and asleep when I heard the music my mother loved. And I could see her dancing all around the kitchen, her laughter echoing behind her all through the house.

I continued listening to her laughter, and suddenly I could smell her delightful cooking. A second later I smelled wood burning and heard the fire crackling. In a flash, I was warming my body and soul in front of our black woodstove. I loved that moment, so I went deeper into my thoughts and waited for memories.

I began smiling from ear to ear as I watched her dancing in my mind's eye. Mesmerized by her joy—a joy that brought me back home in an instant—I opened my eyes. I was amazed at the sense of wholeness and peace of being I felt the moment I remembered her bright light. Still feeling her presence, I closed my eyes again, and there was my twin brother all dressed in his traditional Mexican charro fiesta outfit. I went back into a deeper meditation, so I could hold on to those more vivid thoughts of Mariano a little longer.

I saw Mariano wearing his big black Mexican hat covered with bright, colorful sequins of two eagles and sequins around the large brim. He was wearing his multicolor blanket, known as a *serape,* draped over his shoulder. He looked so serious, but very handsome.

I also had my fiesta outfit. Mama would braid my hair with large red ribbons she rolled under to make big bows that covered my ears like big flowers. I took a look in the mirror, and I looked beautiful with my big red bows. Happy and excited, I would wiggle around to get into my white embroidered blouse with red roses covering the round collar. My skirt was long and red, green, and white, full with a big eagle. The eagle in the front of my skirt appeared to be flying and was covered with sequins that sparked with a rainbow of colors when I moved my skirt from side to side in rhythm to the music.

My brother and I would perform the Mexican hat dance for guests when my parents had special parties. The kitchen and living room came to life, filled with neighbors and friends that lived near and far. I remember all the sounds and smells as if I were still at the party. The music, dancing, cooking food, and lots of kids running around laughing and yelling tickled my heart with happiness. I was laughing out loud when Robert touched me and asked, "Are you all right?"

"Yes," I answered. "I was just dancing with my twin brother." I turned to Robert.

I can still see my mother's smile full of pride when we danced. The guests would remark on how great the twins looked and how wonderfully we danced.

I remember that special birthday for my mama was the last time I felt beautiful—the last day I floated on air with pride. Grammar school started that September, and when it did, my life was immediately turned upside down. I would run up the levee with my stomach upset. My giant would whisper, "Don't worry. I will be with you always."

The music was still in my head when we arrived back at our motor home. The following morning I woke up feeling tired and haunted. I also still felt compelled to find my mama, as my intuition was loud and unyielding. I could hear her voice saying she had something to tell me but that I must visit to hear her message. My bed was warm, and the smell of coffee brewing was cozy. I snuggled deep into my soft, warm bed thinking about Mama and thinking about how I came to realize I was different.

This is what I knew on that morning: I could hear and talk to mama and other spirits. My journey started when I realized I was different, and it all unfolded over time. Now I can talk about intuition and how it shows up in my daily life. Now I do not judge anyone. I see the good in all—the many blessings in every aspect of my life, intuition, and the potential for knowing that grace exist in all beings.

I kept talking and said, "Mama." I have an example that stands out for me when my extrasensory awareness spoke to me. I was driving down a narrow stretch of highway heading home from Reno, Nevada, to Panther Valley. Traffic started to slow down for a car that was stopped on the side of the road. As I passed that car, I saw it was a 1938 black Chevrolet just like the one my father had for years. Fond memories of learning how to drive in the fields on the farm in that old car came flooding in. In between those moments of thought, I could see his face and hear his laughter.

Suddenly, my happy thoughts of him turned to a sick feeling. On a physical level, my stomach felt nauseous. I excused the upset stomach because I was tired from shopping and driving all day. After dinner, I was cleaning the kitchen when I felt his presence again; only this time, I felt sad. All those feelings went to bed with me and came up in a dream that night and the following night. In my dream, I lost something. So I was looking in alleyways, towns, and mountains and felt upset and scared because I could not find what I was looking for.

There was no telephone. Early the next day I drove toward Reno and stopped at the first phone booth I saw. I called several people, hoping to find someone who knew what was going on. Finally, I reach my brother Eddie. He told me Dad was in the hospital, paralyzed and in a coma. Eddie said he had been trying to reach me for three days since Dad had been admitted to the Sacramento Medical Center. All the warning signs of those past three days came crashing in on me, emotionally and physically. I sat down and held my head in my hands, crying and sobbing out loud. "I knew it. I knew it. If only I had listened to my intuition. What if he dies before I can get to Sacramento?" I felt terror in my heart and started to pray. I thought, *Please, Universe, let me make it in time,* because I knew I could heal him.

On my drive to Sacramento, A lady in white appeared, and I heard her sweet voice. "Be calm and stay focused on your driving. Your father is alive and well. He poisoned himself drinking his own urine. He thought he was having a heart attack, so he drank his own urine." A sense of relief washed over me, and the horrifying feeling was gone. That is when I swore I would never doubt my intuition again.

The divine guides you to be able to feel at times and see into other dimensions. Hearing information with a complete understanding of what you are told is pure truth. There is no escape from knowing and seeing other beings; it just is. I personally inherited the privilege of being a psychic medium healer.

Mama I find it interesting that you are contacting me when there was a time you were fearful of me seeing spirits. I can still hear your voice yelling at me as if it were yesterday. "Oh my God, Maria. On your knees and pray so the devil does not take your soul. Hail Mary, Mother of God." Those words came roaring out of your quivering lips.

Remembering back how I slowly raised my head and looked straight into Mama's eyes. They were wide with fear, her face drained of color. Her fear was like an electric shock, shooting though my body, numbing me, scaring me, and demanding I pray. She grabbed me and pushed me down on my knees. With all my strength, I tried to pull away, but her hand held me tight. She swiftly moved behind me, grabbing my shoulders with a paralyzing grip.

With piercing pain around my throat, my heart was beating fast, and I thought I was going to die. It was only a few seconds, but it felt like minutes. Air began to move through my nose, and Mama's prayers were part of the air. She released her grip, and I ran—confused. I could see my mama was afraid of me for some reason. There was so much drama because I told Mama that I had seen a spirit at the foot of the bed.

Memories kept flowing, and I remembered Mama's fear of ghosts, especially on the day my brother and I were running into the house through the kitchen door.

Bang! My brother Eddie and I came through the kitchen yelling, knocking the table out of our way with the bench as the door slammed behind us. The door hit so hard that it echoed through the long, narrow kitchen.

"Mama, Mama." Eddie pushed past me, yelling in a high-pitched voice filled with fear. "I need my clothes. There is a lady outside. Hurry! She saw me naked. The lady is standing by the

water faucet behind the house." Eddie was shivering and pushing
Mama with both his hands toward the bedroom for his clothes.

Mama turned around and reached Eddie's shoulder, pressing
him closer against her side and trying to calm and comfort him.
I finally caught up to him. Mama quickly yelled. "Slow down.
No running through the kitchen."

I was still watching Mama calm Eddie when I noticed she
was shaking her head side to side and saying no. Immediately,
I knew she did not believe Eddie, so I started jumping up and
down yelling. "There is a lady with a little girl outside."

Mama replied. "There is nobody outside." She grabbed our
hands tight and led us back outside to show us there was nobody there. My brother and I looked at each other in silence.
We thought the lady and child had just moved to the other side
of the yard.

I yelled loudly. "Mama, we saw her."

In a stern voice, Mama said, "Stay outside and play; I do not
want to hear about this again."

We were scared, but Mama forced us to play outside. That
did not make us feel safe. We did not move. We stood so still we
could hear our hearts beating.

We reluctantly went around to the front of the house. I
think we were more scared of Mama than the lady and child.

I am still amazed at the opportunity my brother and I had
to see with our spiritual eyes. When I look back at that day
when I ran through our kitchen and think about what we witnessed, it still amazes me. Mama never believed we saw a lady
with a small child at her side, but we did indeed see the spirits of
the two of them. During dinnertime, we wanted to talk about
the lady, but Mama quickly shut us up.

That night, something woke me in the middle of my sleep.

I started to rub my eyes and sat up, trying to focus in the dark. I saw what looked like a figure in front of me, but it was too dark to see clearly. The figure moved closer to my bed, but I still could not make out who it was. I called out. "Mama, is that you?" The words had barely come out of my mouth when I saw a man wearing a long, white robe floating just above the floor. I froze for a moment, but my eyes continued to focus on his white hair and mustache, which had a bluish white glow. I felt blood pumping through my heart into my ears. I closed my eyes, and this time I remembered my mama's voice praying for me. I started praying out loud for God to save me. I said, "I promise not to be bad ever again."

I grabbed the blanket and yanked it over my head. I still remember thinking, *Mama is right. That man spirit is going to get me for sure.* Stories of evil spirits flooded my head like icy waves. With each breath the waves of fear seemed endless.

Then I heard a voice. "Do not fear me, I am here for you. I am here to help you whenever you need help. When you are afraid, listen for the sound of my voice; it will be a soft whisper."

I did not know who and what to believe—what the message spirit said or what my mama said. All I know is that fear would sneak in my soul and weave its way for a short time into my fun, loving, peaceful, happy days of playing with spirits.

Now I can laugh about the time I was around six years old and did not know there was a world outside the levee near my house. It was a time of discovery and amazing fun, free of restrictions. Later, I would realize that rules were waiting around the corner that would change my life. However, on the levee, it was a time of discovery and fun, living free of restrictions with my make believe giant.

Now I realize that my first rule was to fear God. If I dared misbehave, God would see and punish me with grave results. Mama would say that if I dared to raise my hand or voice at her, my hand would turn to stone.

Mama's fear had an effect on me, because at times I felt self-conscious, thinking God was watching me. I did not know what could happen to me if I did something that was considered bad, because Mama and God may not approve. I now know that being afraid of not having approval created the need for approval.

I was around eleven years old when an overwhelming feeling of being an outsider around others became even stronger. I did not have a clue as to why I was different, and it took me years of chasing approval to find myself.

I was still in meditation maintain my own space when all of a sudden all four of my dogs jumped on the bed. They started barking and licking all over me, telling me it was time to get up. Reluctantly, I got up, walked to front of the motor home, sat on the couch, and drank my coffee. I was determined to find my mamas grave site. I picked up my phone and called directory assistance to ask for the number of the Catholic Church in Woodland Ca. I thanked the lady for giving me the number and the name of the person I needed to contact. After twenty minutes on hold and being passed around, I finally reached the person in charge of the grave sites.

It was midmorning when I pulled out of the RV park and headed for Woodland to find my mama and have a conversation with her. I had not been back to her grave since the day we buried her in December 1963.

On my second day in Woodland, I drove by the ranch at Elkhorn Ferry where I grew up. I decided to stop and visit my old house and sit on the levee with my giant again. The land was empty and plowed under, and our house was no longer there. I felt sad that it was all gone. All the fruit trees Dad had planted, the white fence, the big barn, even our driveway—it was all gone. Sadness swept through my whole being as I wondered what had happen and when it had been torn down. My father had worked long hours building a bathroom and other comforts. It was wonderful having inside plumbing and not having to go outside to the outhouse and worry about spiders and the scary nights. We no longer had to take baths in a round galvanized tub with hot water poured from the wood stove. I loved taking a bath in the large, white bathtub that had claws for feet.

I pulled off the road and parked the car where our driveway had been at one time. I walked up to the Sacramento River levee where I spent so much time as a young girl, and occasionally as an adult, visiting with my giant.

I found the perfect place to sit, so I went back to the car for my blanket. I spread my blanket and settled into a comfortable position. The sun was warm; it was not long before I was transported back to the time when I was a small child.

My favorite place on the levee was facing the house, sitting on my giant's eyebrow. Here I would lie down with my arms stretched out, enjoying the sun and the smell and feel of the grass.

Magic always happened when I got hot. Out of nowhere, a soft breeze would blow over me, keeping me cool and safe. When it was cold, the sun would keep me warm. At different times butterflies would land on me, close to my hands. This spot on the levee was my place to retreat, to daydream, or to look for answers when I was overwhelmed as a child and even as an adult. I would lie on the soft grass of the riverbank daydreaming. I loved looking at all the different colored auras around plants, trees, and people.

Feeling the earth under my body and taking in all the sweet smells of grass, water, dirt, wild flowers, and different fragrances the wind carried awakened all my senses. I would stare up at the fluffy clouds that created angels, people, animals, faces, and faraway countries to visit.

Watching brilliant color moving around trees, plants, animals, and people brought wonder into my day. As a child I would often wish, *What if I could be just like the earth?* And I wondered if I had color around my body. Adults and friends dismissed my ideas and visions as wild imagination or said I looked at the world through rose-colored glasses. I was all right with that, because for me it was real—and still is.

I would pretend the earth was a living, moving giant and I lived on his eyebrow balcony surveying the universe from my perch. I chose his eyebrow because I could see the entire world from there. The eyebrow was the part of the levee that faced my house. Right below his chest, around the heart, all the angels, spirits, and entities played and tickled my heart with their wings.

After my short stop on the levee of Sacramento River at Elkhorn Ferry, I finally pulled into the cemetery at Woodland and parked. The wind was not blowing as hard, but it was still breezy and cold.

With instructions in hand, I quickly found the row number and walked down a couple of rows, passing her plot twice before I found her small headstone. I yelled out loud, "Here it is," but I felt sorrow to see that her headstone was so small and overgrown with grass. I also noticed the headstone of my brother's son, Mariano Jr., directly above Mama's little stone. His stone was grand with a baseball player on the side, beautifully carved. My brother's son was wrongfully killed, and his ashes were resting with Mama.

Kneeling, I cleared the weeds off the headstone. I became overwhelmed and started to cry, asking Mama's forgiveness for not visiting sooner. I repeated in Spanish, "Please, please forgive me." I was sobbing so hard I became sick to my stomach. I felt so guilty for not having visited in so many years. I had no idea why I now had that hard pull to be here. I thought maybe there were unresolved issues I had not looked at, but these feelings were new to me as I stood there that day.

I sat on the wet grass next to her, and then I moved on top of her grave and laid my whole body over her. I needed a hug and to feel close to her. I closed my eyes, and I could feel the warm embrace of her loving arms. I stayed in this position for a while. Time stood still, so I had no idea how long I lay over her on the wet grass. Then I sat up and began a conversation with her. I could feel her presence next to me, and her voice was as I remembered it. It was way beyond my expectations to hear her voice. It was as if we were talking on the porch at our old house.

I started the conversation by telling Mama how my life had gone since I last saw her in the hospital as she took her last breath. Still crying, I told her that I wished it was me that had died that day and that I was willing to trade places with her when she took her last breath.

After a time, I continued my conversation, speaking sometimes softly and sometimes loudly. I explained that the first half of my life had been extremely difficult and filled with fear, a lack of identity, a lack of self-esteem, abuse, physical injuries, and hiding behind masks. I told her that I had followed the rules and worked hard at being a good woman. I loved and obeyed the man of the house and kept my feelings inside me.

I said out loud, "Mama, growing up you told me when I was young that my role as a woman would be to do whatever was expected of me. I remember what you said: 'Always please your man no matter what.' I tried to be that woman, but I could not. I did not like being told what to do and never being accepted or never being good enough. Even worse, when I allowed them to brutalize me under the flag of love and loyalty, I did what was expected of me."

I stopped and asked myself why I was arguing with my mama's spirit—silly me.

I started to explain to Mama what I had learned and then I heard her say, "Silence, Maria. I know what happened in your life. I was there when you could not endure any longer. I gave you guidance to rediscover yourself. I want you to use your love and knowledge to help those in your world and those of us who have crossed over."

"Mama, I promise to write, teach, and help people heal themselves within. I will help everybody to see their own identities, the power to choose the lives they desire, and the power that every person has within to heal."

I heard Mama tell me that many people who have crossed over need help giving messages to loved ones. I promised that whenever someone needed me to send a message to loved ones, I would help when called upon.

Mama reminded me that I was born sensitive and lived between two worlds—ours and that of the soul that moves over to the other side. I had one foot on earth and the other in a different dimension. I told her that I would help others learn they have great value and much love they can radiate. I told Mama I knew how to help because I had learned and studied for many years. I learned how to love myself, how to be at peace, and how to become whole. I also learned that I am a piece of the universe; therefore, I am one with the world and the universe.

Still crying and feeling deeply emotional, I started thinking of my family. I just let those emotions continue to bubble up. After I had stopped crying, I was surprised that I had such clarity of my life mission.

I felt I needed to leave a gift, so I searched my purse to find something meaningful. Hanging on my purse was a jade gourd a friend of mine had given me with love. With my keys, I made a deep hole and left my gift with gratitude and love.

As I stood up straight, my last words that day were of gratitude that Mama had beckoned me there. I said, "I am honored and pleased beyond words that you can see me today and every day."

I left and slowly drove back to our motor home with a mind full of both sad and happy memories. I wanted to remember all my childhood, but I could not see or hear everything at that time.

When I arrived at the motor home, I was busy taking care of my dogs and Garfield, my huge cat. I made dinner, cleaned up, and moved to the back room for some quiet. It had been a good day full of fabulous wonder, and visiting my mama was the icing on the cake. I felt proud of myself and of my mama.

Upon awaking early in the morning, I discovered that Robert and all our animals were still sound asleep. It was the perfect time to meditate. During my deep meditation, I began telling Mama about my adventures and how I had become whole. I told her how I had rediscovered that little girl who lived and played on the levee of the Sacramento River banks with her giant.

I was only a few minutes into my meditation when out of nowhere there was a spirit in front me telling me she needed to contact her daughter. I replied, "As soon as I can find her, I will give your message if she wants to hear it."

Sometimes spirits ambush me in the middle of a store or at the checkout counter of a restaurant or movie theater. Sometimes they ambush me in my own house. I was born with the talent of having clairvoyance. That comes with a wide knowledge. I not only see spirits, but I am also connected to earth and the universe. I always know what is going on before someone says anything. Now my mama has told me that being a medium and healer is my strongest talent and that I should help those who ask.

I started laughing out loud, remembering when I was young, without rules and wild as a jackrabbit. The whole levee alongside the Sacramento River was my playground. I would run down the levee with my arms extended, flapping them as fast as I could and fly. Robert asked me what was so funny. I answered, "Me."

"Good for you; tell me what was so funny," he said

I started to tell him about how I would fly. Then all of sudden I started slowly jumping up and down in a dancing rhythm, laughing and crying at the same time. I lifted my right hand in a motion for Robert to wait until I stopped laughing.

Before I gave him an answer, my thoughts jumped, and I heard myself saying out loud, "My visit with Mama."

Robert said, "What did you say?"

I told Robert I was sorry. I said, "I will tell you later, but right now my thoughts are on what happened at Mama's grave."

I continued thinking about my conversation with Mama at her grave. I asked her why she did not love me as she loved my brothers and why she took better care of them. I wanted to know why I was left alone to run wild and why nobody cared where I was or if I was safe. I sat quietly for a long time, and then I heard her voice as if she were standing next to me. "No, no, Maria.

That is not true; they had no self-esteem, and their macho ways needed more attention. You walked with angels, and your soul was and still is the purest expression of love. You were not bound by physical forms or fleeting emotions. I saw you strong and connected to the universe, talking to angels and entities."

"No, Mama, I only had my giant." I waited a moment and continued my sentence. "Well you are right. I did have spirits to play with, but I really needed you to hold me and tell me you loved me."

Mama replied, "I am sorry your experiences were colored with the pain of thinking no one accepted you or that you were not loved. Maria, I have always loved you. I just thought you knew that. You have always known love and enjoyed completeness. When you played with the earth and with its many entities which make up love, you just got lost for a while."

I went on to say, "Mama, there are so many things you did not tell me growing up. I have more questions about spirits and why they scared you at one time."

She answered, "Be patient. I will reveal it all when the time is right. When I visit, you will feel a chill, and your head will tingle."

I asked her, "Please tell me why you were afraid of me when I was around ten years old. You thought I was a witch."

"Not now. I want you to find a quiet place to remember when you forgot that you were one with the universe," she replied.

I laughed so hard I wet my pants. All this time I did not know my mama loved me. I had buried that hurtful piece of information because it was painful to think that my own mama did not love me. At that moment, sitting on the levee I remembered when and why I lost that piece of me.

After my early childhood, I ran into another world outside my house and yard waiting to change my life. My first horrible upheaval was when I had to attend school. It was there that I learned to be afraid. Grammar school was like being transported to a strange planet. I didn't know English, so I could not understand the language. However, I learned it in time, and having kids to talk to and play with was great.

It was painful to sit in a desk for hours. I wiggled around in my chair and talked to kids around my desk; sometimes I would daydream. The teacher would point her finger at me and say in a loud voice, "Sit down and be quiet," or "No day dreaming in this class; go stand in the corner of the room." She continued, "Maria, quiet! Did you not understand no talking in class? I warned you about talking. Put your hands on your desk."

Her ruler smacked the back of my hand. It stung, but I refused to cry in front of the class. I held my breath, tightened my jaw, and waited for the next smack and banishment the corner of the room.

I know how my classmate John felt one day when he was made to stand in the corner with a dunce cap. That day I cried for him, and today I cry and feel so humiliated for myself. John never misbehaved again.

I asked, "Mama, answer just one more question."

She said, "Just one more."

"Do you remember when I had nightmares and walked in my sleep, and you thought I was dancing with witches?" I asked her. "Remember the day you took me into your bedroom and walked me to the window? Do you remember that you pulled back the curtain to show me the half-driven nails protruding from the window frame? I stared at the nails in horror while listening to your voice. I was so frighten I really did not hear you. I just sat on the edge of the bed staring at the white lacy curtains stuck on the nails."

I heard her answer. "Maria, I was afraid you would open the window and get out. Your father and I nailed the windows and moved the lock up high to keep you safe. I had no knowledge about sleepwalking, and I thought the witches wanted you. On earth I did not understand many things, especially about superstition alongside religion."

"After that," I said, "I suffered. I became separated from believing in what I saw and from feeling that I belonged on my giant's eyebrow as part of the wholeness of universe. Doubt crept into my soul and weaved through all parts of my life for a long time."

Tears continued to run down my cheeks as I explained to her. "Oh, Mama," I cried. "I was so young I thought being a witch was bad and evil because witches were the ones with the power to do harm. The only image of a witch I had was a woman with a long nose, black hat, long nails, and a loud, scary voice. In your stories, if children were bad, she would fly in and scoop them away forever. Mama, I was only six or seven years old. I thought the dark evil or witch might summon me. That day in your bedroom I changed in such a small way I was not aware until it became so all-encompassing that I did not recognize myself. One day I stood in front of the mirror and pretended to be anybody else. It felt good to escape and pretend to be somebody else for a while."

"Oh, Maria," she answered. "I was the one showing you and whispering in your ear to buy books that would light your path."

"I heard you, Mama," I said, "but it took me awhile to completely trust my intuition and what I heard. When can we talk again? Oh, before you leave, I want to let you know that later in my life I realized, because of your superstitions, that my fear of demons, witches, and spirits was an illusion of my insecure mind."

"Do not be so hard on yourself," she argued, "You were just a small child when all this happened."

"I understand, Mama," I replied, "but I recall when you and Dad thought I was not a normal girl. Both of you told me you thought I was crazy. When you spoke about me to family or friends, you told them that I had a head injury, and air got into my head causing me to see things and act crazy. Remember when we were playing hide-and-seek blindfolded, and I ran into the corner of the wood stove? I hit that sharp edge so hard it cut a long gash on my forehead. I got scared only after I took off my blindfold and saw the blood. That's when I started screaming and crying. Still crying, I heard Dad telling you to get an egg. I was jumping and crying as his fingers started pushing on my forehead pinching my cut closed. Then he cracked open the egg and took out the inside skin of the shell to put over my cut. When the egg skin dried, the bleeding stopped. His eggshell skin was the perfect Band-Aid. I heard you whisper to Dad, 'Air got in her head, and that is going to make her crazy.'

"I am sure that day your words planted the seed that something was wrong with me. For years I thought air had gotten into my brain through my forehead, and that caused me to be intuitive and not right in the head. Mama, tell me about that day."

"Yes I will, but not today," she promised

"But, Mama," I pleaded, "I need an answer, please."

I find it interesting that to this day my brothers still tell the story of how I became crazy. I am amazed at the entire silly episode that happened to me as a child. It was an episode that

puzzle I did not know; something felt wrong.

The next night it was the same dream, except this time I flew over a huge American flag and small flags alongside the flowers. The next morning I did not say anything to anybody about the dream, but it bothered me. I felt sad and had a heavy feeling around my heart and an upset stomach.

Then my fears were realized. On the fourth night, my parents received a telegram that our neighbor's son Harvey, who was like one of my brothers, had been shot while on duty with the Marine Corps in San Diego, California. He was in critical condition.

Harvey was a tall, handsome, lanky boy with dark hair and very fair skin. He lived with his mother in a railroad boxcar that had been made into a home. Several cars were joined together to create a large house. His mother had moved in with her brother's family, who worked for the railroad. They lived in their boxcar home alongside the railroad, two miles from our house.

Harvey loved all of our family, and he kind of adopted us. He stayed with us most of the time. When he enlisted in the Marines, he listed my parents as his emergency family contact. I had a little girl's crush on him, and my entire family loved him as one of our boys.

We got busy making sandwiches and snacks for our trip to San Diego, hoping to see him before he died. The drive was long and stressful, and we prayed we would make it in time. I prayed loudly to make sure I was heard.

I was sad that I did not get to say good-bye and tell him my birthday was on the twenty-fifth. Several days later at his funeral, the flag that was draped on his coffin was given to my parents.

Driving through the base gates to the hospital, I saw rows

and rows of all the flowers I had seen in my dream before he died. When I saw the landscape and flowers, I gasped because I knew immediately I had been on these grounds as our car passed down the long road to the hospital. I kept this information to myself; I dared not to say a word about what I felt and knew in my heart. I knew I had visited this Marine base for the past three nights.

There would be many other dreams that spoke to me of upcoming events. They were in color, loud, happy, silly, or haunting. The more confusion I had during the day about emotions, problems, or fears, the more I would dream. I was blessed with dreams that shone the light on my daily life to help me to solve problems.

I was still too young to recognize the importance of my dreams and distinguish which ones were premonitions. Some dreams helped me to understand wisdom and better myself.

On another Saturday night, I once again woke up from a sound sleep screaming that my twin brother was in trouble and needed help. I could see boys beating on my brother. I felt the pain when the first blow hit his head. I could hear and feel glass crashing on my face. It felt wet.

I woke my parents up with my screams, and while I was explaining my dream, our neighbor came over and knocked on the front door. My dad opened the door, and our neighbor had a piece of paper with a message from the police telling us Mariano was in the hospital. Shortly afterward, a police officer came to the door to tell us that my brother had been at a dance when a fight broke out. He had been beaten on his head and face.

An officer explained to us that we were needed at the hospital and then to the police station to sign paperwork. They also explained that after the hospital released my brother, Mariano would be needed at the police station to give his statement and identify the assailants.

We parked our car near the emergency room. I went into the emergency room desk and asked about my brother, and the nurse pointed to the corner. I quickly walked in front of my parents and pulled back the curtain to his bed. I stood still and stared at him before I could say a word; his wounds were just like in my dreams. I walked away as my parents stood by his bed. I felt uneasy because only hours earlier I felt the pain and saw the blood on my face. I found my voice and told Mama that it was just like in my dream. She became upset with me and asked me to wait outside in the waiting room.

My foot was twitching fast. I was nervous. I did not understand where the thoughts came from, or if it was good or bad. I did not have control of what I saw or heard in my dreams. I wanted my dreams to stop. I was going to hell for sure, according to my parents. My whole body filled up with pain and guilt that I had done something to cause it.

When we got to the car, Mama asked me how I could have done this to my brother. I tried to explain that it had been a dream, and I had nothing to do with it. I promised I would never have these dreams again. There were many more dreams, but I kept them to myself.

I prayed long and hard not to dream and to forget them if I did have dreams. One interesting phenomena that I recognized around this same time was an awareness I had of what people were going to say before they spoke. I knew things without knowing why.

I could see wonderful colors around everything; I saw spirits, ghosts, and entities. I would sit on the Sacramento levee with all my thoughts and wonder if anyone else was like me.

I felt lonely and separated from the rest of my family and the kids at school. My emotions were confused, and I could not help but wonder if I was not whole mentally. My summers passed quickly, and I was happily waiting for high school start. I had visions of wonderful days and kids. I knew I would make new friends and find somebody like me. My dreams had stopped, and I spent a lot of time on my beloved levee waiting for a new beginning.

CHAPTER 3

High School

On the first day high school the bus was full of kids from our old school and other kids from a wider area who were also assigned to our high school in Woodland, California. I was excited. I was up early to get ready for school. I wore my best dress, polished my shoes, and tied new ribbons in my hair. The minute I saw kids from school I felt awful. They looked at me with a look I did not recognize, but one that was not friendly. Nobody said a word, but my intuition spoke loudly that I was not welcome or liked.

My high school was large, with about eight hundred students. At first sight, I noticed their clothes and shoes were so different from what I had ever seen. The hairstyles were short, and I quickly felt like a freak.

I walked home slowly and wondered how I could change my looks and, more importantly, how I was going to convince my parents to pay for a haircut and new clothes.

My father was not happy about me going to high school. He believed I should not even be in school, because I was to be married and did not need an education. My parents did not have extra money to buy new shoes or fancy shirts. I just changed my hair and began wearing it down without bows.

The following days at school I walked with my head down so I would not see how the kids would sneer and make fun of me. Then a boy named Byron looked at me with a most beautiful smile. I was so hungry for a friendly person that I imagined I was in love and drew hearts with his name in the middle. Well, I wasn't really in love, but I did like him. I was so hungry for affection.

In spite of loving his attention, my intuition (that inner voice) spoke to me and showed me an array of problems I would face with him in my life if I continued on my path. I dismissed that inner voice and the angel message and yelled at the universe. "I do not believe you about Byron. You do not understand I need somebody to love and accept me."

With tears rolling down my face and with my hands clutched, I vowed I would follow my heart. I heard a soft voice from an angel telling me, "Maria, do not be ignorant and create a hard, abusive life that will last for years. Remember we will always be with you, and you carry with you the wisdom of the universe. Listen to your inner voice."

I opened my eyes and looked at my wristwatch. I saw I had been sitting for hours on the soft carpet of grass on my beloved levee thinking about the conversation I had with Mama. I walked to edge of the water and put my feet into the water. I continued my conversation for a little longer. Then I got back to my car and continue my visit with my mama, at her grave. I can't say how the whispers of my angels came to warn me about Byron being on his way to see me. It started in the middle of a hot summer night. I heard a knock on my bedroom window. It was Byron, motioning me to open the window. He liked me a lot. I found that flattering and welcomed his attention. I was not his girlfriend, but I did enjoy talking to him at school. He would come to my house and even walked the twelve miles from Woodland, California, to Elkhorn Ferry where I lived on a farm.

I opened the window, and Byron's first words were, "Hurry, come with me. I am running away, and I came to get you."

"What?!" I wondered aloud.

He quickly put his hand over my mouth. "Sh, not so loud. You are going to wake everyone." He took his hand off my mouth.

"Are you out of your mind coming here and scaring me like that? No, I will not run away. Why do you need to run away?" I asked

His face looked worried and flushed. He whispered, "My friend who works at the pizza place came up with the idea of robbing the place at closing time."

I covered my face with my hands, and my fingers clutched my hair as I shook my head no. I took a step back and stopped him in the middle of his words. "Oh no. How could you?"

He looked at me with such a loving but hurt stare and continued his story. He swallowed hard, and his hands shook. "My friend and I thought it was a great way to start a life together with his girlfriend and mine. He grabbed my hand, pulling me hard toward the window and saying, "Hurry, let's go."

My voice grew loud when I said, "No, I will not run away with you or anybody else."

Byron started to plead. "Please, come with me now. My friend and his girlfriend are waiting for us in his car."

I firmly said, "No, it is wrong to steal."

Again, Byron started pulling on my hand, saying, "Hurry, come on."

I pulled my hand back, yelling, "Hey, listen to me. You have to call the police and turn yourself in. Tell your friend to leave or turn him in too."

"Are you crazy? I am not going to do that to my friend," he argued.

"Byron," I said, "I promise if you turn yourself in for me, I will stick by you."

He was pacing back and forth, talking louder and repeating, "I cannot lose you. I love you and want you to marry me. We robbed the pizza place so we could get married."

I felt flattered and angry at the same time. After a short pause, I heard my voice saying, "I will marry you if you turn yourself in tonight. I promise. Let's call the police." I do not know where that promise came from, but I could not believe I said it.

That memory me made feel uneasy, so I got up and walked around and took a long look at where my old house had once stood. I walked down to the water. The smell of the wet levee and the river was refreshing and beautiful. The current was moving the water fast. Small whitecaps appeared on the top of the water, making appear as if it were dancing.

I was skipping rocks on the water when I heard that familiar whisper. "Maria, you must finish your thoughts of Byron."

I said I would as soon as I finished playing on the banks with the water hitting my toes.

As the water tickled my toes, I closed my eyes and took some deep breaths and asked Mama to help me remember everything that had happened that night.

We did not have a telephone, so I woke up my brother and asked him to follow me into my room. I explained the problem to him and asked him to walk to the neighbor's house and use his phone to call the police. It took the police awhile before they arrived to arrest Byron. During that time, we talked about our future and what we would do once he got out. Deep in my soul I knew I should not marry Byron, but I had made a promise at a moment when my emotions were jumbled up.

My parents woke when the police arrived, so I walked into their bedroom. I explained that we had called the police and that Byron was turning himself in because he had stolen some money.

My father was glad and thought that was going to be the last of Byron. I looked out window and saw the policeman handcuffing him and ran out as they put him in the back seat of the car. As the patrol car pulled away, I could see Byron in the back seat looking back at me. It broke my heart to see him handcuffed and arrested.

I immediately felt responsible, because I had talked him into turning himself over to the police. In that moment I felt guilt and remorse, which created an invisible bond between us.

He was given one year in juvenile hall. We started writing each other, and I would run to the mailbox to get the mail. My father gave me such a hard time every time I received a letter that I started defending Byron.

I was walking back to the house from the mailbox when a car drove into our yard. I slowly watch this big woman get out and ask for me. She introduced herself as Mrs. Bennett. She worked with the juvenile system to help first-time offenders. She liked Byron and helped him with the letters he wrote me and gave him money for stamps. She drove all the way to my house to talk to me about how I could help him. She told me that Byron touched her heart when he told her how he met me.

Byron told her that when he saw me standing by my locker

for the first time, he knew I was born to be his. She explained that from that moment he saw me in that hall it was true love at first sight. She asked me to please answer his letters so that it would help him settle down and stop being so hostile. At that moment, I flashed back to the handcuffs and felt that under the flag of love and loyalty I owed him. I politely told her I would write.

After our conversation, as Mrs. Bennett was getting into her car to leave, she told me that she thought if I kept my promise to marry him, he would buckle down and get out sooner for good behavior. I believed his life was in my hands. That day, as I watched the dust settle after she drove off, I promised myself that I'd answer all his letters.

After dinner, I told my father about Mrs. Bennett's visit and explained that I had promised her I would marry Byron. My father went ballistic, slamming his hand on the table and yelling. "You will not marry that thief."

I did not understand why he would not allow me to marry him. I was sitting in a pool of my own tears, asking myself, "Why me?"

My father's hard words were still ringing in my head: "Stay away from Byron."

One year later, Byron came to collect on my promise. Again, I did not listen to my intuition, though it screamed at me so loudly it hurt. The pain I felt was as if I were being squeezed by a vise grip. I felt as if I had no air in my lungs or on the top of my stomach. The pain was horrible and stayed with me for months. I did not want to get married, but a promise was a promise. I did not know how to say no. After all, he loved me so much that he went to jail for me. He was free, and I became his prisoner. I felt shame when I told my parents Byron was out of juvenile hall, and it was time to get married. My father got drunk and went on a rampage, saying no and telling me to get out of his house.

I got married, and my obligation to honor my husband was horrible and painful. I forced myself to keep my promise regardless of what I wanted, even though it was beyond abusive and he tortured me. Dreams came back with a loud voice, showing me a way out of this abusive relationship.

I woke up in a sweat from a dream where bad guys with guns were chasing me and I was running for my life when I heard a loud clear voice. "Get out, or he will kill you." I woke up and ignored the dream, convincing myself it was just a dream. Afraid to sleep, I was exhausted and could not see what was in front of me. I convinced myself by saying, "I have no place to go, no money. How can I take care of all six of my kids?" Again, that inner voice yelled, "Get out." Leave Byron. Overwhelmed with conflict, fear and emotional crises, I felt paralyzed. Where could I go where he would not find me and my six babies? I curled up and cried in desperation and called out to universe to help me.

Many times I had reached a crossroads where choices seemed to involve the risk of facing the unknown versus the safety and comfort of all that I came to trust or know.

I did, over time, learn to love Byron, in the beginning it was not always bad. Alcohol and drugs played a big part in the evil person he became. Once I found the strength to stand up to him, he left. It would be years later before I mourned the marriage and the man I wanted him to be. Even once I was free to live my own life on my terms, I still at times have trouble crossing that road of the unknown.

The cold water on my toes brought me back. I felt my bottom was wet and cold. I got up off the levee and walked back to my car. I drove back to my motor home without much thought about what I had been shown. I was cold, and the sun was warm in my car. I enjoyed listening to music on my drive back.

I woke up early, and my mama was sitting on the edge of my bed. My sleepy eyes flew open with excitement.

"Mama, you came; tell me what was so important to travel back in time to when I was seventeen," I said.

"Maria, we traveled to remind you of your talent of being a sensitive and able to see spirits, angels, and entities. The keen intuition you have of seeing auras and your ability to speak with all spirits has set you apart from others for the betterment of mankind," she responded.

"I was proud you did not let your hard life put your brilliant light out and glad you found your true self to do the work you were born to do," she continued. "I gave you a guild to help you hear when you tuned out your inner voice. Do you remember when you cried and yelled at the universe to show you a way out of your marriage and later the wrecking yard where you lived? Within a few days, the answer was revealed to you, and you acted on it. You were back in California where you found freedom."

"Mama, I do remember," I told her.

From that point on, I began searching for books to find my way back to my giant and my angels' voices. That was my first step after years of needing everybody and anybody to tell me I was worthy of being loved.

"Dreams were first on my list to overcome, because they scared me," I explained to Mama.

"I know, Maria," she answered. "Tell me how you overcame old fears and learned what the dreams were telling you."

I found the courage to take classes on the wonderful world of dreams and the paranormal at American River College in Sacramento, California. I bought lots of books from many authors about dreams. I finished the courses and continued to unravel my intuition. My first year of classes helped validate my own inner voice. My inner knowing began to surface again. This time, I enjoyed my soul's voice.

I began learning how to listen to symbols instead of words, which helped me realize my inner god. I heard my guide's voice once again. Those words empowered me to open my eyes. This was a lifetime gift offering me the understanding of how negative judgment was killing my inner truth.

"Truth can be a powerful catalyst. Once I was free of your words and ideas, Mama, my life was renewed," I told her.

"Mama, I now see that in the beginning, fresh from the womb, I was not honored as a perfect, creative expression of my divine right to be whole. I was assigned a role of what a woman should be and controlled through fear and superstition," I said to Mama. "Thank you for sharing all this information. I have something to share with you. I am so proud of being your daughter."

My mama said good-bye for now and assured me she would come back soon. I took a long, deep breath and let it out slowly through my mouth to relax. I was in a state of grace from having visited with my mama. After a few minutes, I said to myself in a soft whisper, "There is so much programming in humans' lives."

By now I was exhausted and sat in my warm car with the sun shining through my front window. My eyes gazed on the leaves dancing in the sky as I laid my seat back as far as it would go. It was a perfect, quiet place. I closed my eyes when affirmations past by in a quick a memory. It was not long before I fell asleep saying, "I will talk with you soon, Mama, and thank you."

I must have been more tired than I thought, because a dream woke me up. I looked at my wristwatch. I had only been sleeping twenty minutes. I did not sit up, so I could remember my dream. I asked myself what my dream was saying to me.

Just then, I heard a soft voice saying, "Dreams are the gateway to intuition. Be still, and you will remember why this dream happened in such a short sleep. Then I remembered dreams were my first gateway to my intuition. Dreams pushed me to remember who I was and, most important, who I was not.

CHAPTER 4

Validation of My Intuition

I was taught to suppress those feelings that were commonly regarded by my parents and society as negative, such as intuition. Learning to pretend to be somebody other than what I felt, I allowed myself to believe that intuitive, spiritual healers were, in one way or another, evil, silly, wrong, and/or against God. I buried my intuition and dreamed because I was afraid and I thought I was crazy. I was lost and didn't know who to be, so for a time, I was the great pretender.

As I was thinking back and weaving thoughts and memories of times past, Eleanor crossed my mind. My grammar school friend Eleanor was somewhat like me. On one level, we knew we could see and feel each other. We did not talk much about our feelings because we were afraid we would be overheard. There were times when we would hide behind her house, or mine, and talk about how we loved the ability to see and hear what others could not. It was our secret. We loved spending time together; then one day she was gone. I was devastated. I could feel her presence, and I tried to reach her with telepathy. I closed my eyes and imagined myself dialing her phone number. I would watch the telephone line and send my message to her phone. I did get a flash of her being all right.

The story I heard at school was that her mother feared for her life and fled during the night with her two children. Eleanor's father was known to drink and had a bad temper. I saw him when we would visit at her house, but I did not really talk to him. He grew asparagus on his small ranch. All the kids in school lived on farms, and our parents worked for big farmers or had their own small farms.

Gossip was wild, and I did not know what was true or made up. One story was that the neighbors reported gunshots and yelling coming from their house. The police were told Mr. Gomez had a gun. He was going to kill the family and anyone else who interfered.

The story was active and went on for several weeks and then finally stopped. The last I heard was that her dad left his farm months later. I missed my friend a lot and felt the pain of not knowing what had happened to her. I still think about her and wonder if she is alive and well.

I would dream about her, and I could hear her small voice. It sounded like a whisper from a distant place. She would say to me, "Maria, dreams are leading you back to your soul. Start trusting your dreams and recognize your special guide, who will lead you back to paying attention. You are not paying attention. You are in denial about what you are being shown."

I woke up and spoke out loud. "Do you mean my dreams are me talking to myself?!"

It was not surprising that I buried my creative intuitive nature so deep. Eleanor's whisper was so faint, but I heard her say that all beings, including me, have intuition and an aura. I heard her say, "Not to worry; you will find the way back to that place of unity with the universe and myself."

I did not hear her voice again.

I yelled, "No I won't," and raised a fist high in the air, waving it at the universe. I was so wounded that I could not and did not want to add to my pain by listening to dreams or to my own identity and inner voice.

I left it that way for years until out of now where I had the idea of going back to read my diary. I was not sure if I could locate the box in which I stored my artwork, poems, and diary.

I found only one diary I had written when I was around fourteen. I cleaned it off. It was locked, and the key was not in the box, so I pick up some scissors and broke open the lock.

I opened it slowly, almost afraid to read it. The first page said, "Dear diary, Why am I so different, and why am I not liked?" I took a deep breath and continued reading.

"I do not understand why all I hear is 'Maria is crazy. Who does she think she is? She is so stupid. She dresses awful and has no talent. She will never amount to anything.'" I saw my pages stained, and I remembered that as I was writing, my tears hit the diary and blurred the ink. That was it. I then remembered how I'd tossed my pen across the bed and said to myself, "I cannot even write without messing it up."

I was angry and sad, so I closed my book and cried for what seemed like forever. Then I got up and said, "That is not me." I turned to the last page, and it read, "I am not sure who I am yet, but that is not me."

My own words, mixed in with others' ideas of who I should be, made wounds that help me bury my true self. It contributed to the destruction of my self-esteem, which helped to close down my intuition. There were also other factors that scared me into shutting down my spiritual eyes and my beliefs.

My biggest nightmare was that I was crazy, and doctors

would come and take me away to a hospital for insane people. I had seen this on television. My parents always threatened to put me away if I did not behave in an acceptable manner.

I thought the men in white coats would show up and take me away. I lay on my stomach behind the door where I could see and hear the whispering about me.

My father was a quiet man. It was my mama whom I heard say, "But if she hears voices, she could be schizophrenic." I stretched my neck to hear because I had never heard that word—*schizophrenic.*

My imagination ran wild. It was awful and so scary that I just wanted to disappear. I was sorry I was hiding and heard what they were talking about. I promised myself to be good and keep things to myself. Not wanting to be judged, I started keeping secrets. I closed my diary and thought, *What a sad, confused little girl.*

I kept one foot on the side of my own beliefs, because I knew my soul's voice. My other foot was on the side where the fear of my mama and friends helped shape doubt and caused my outward behavior to be different. I did not know in the beginning how to balance the two, so I felt I was on a teeter-totter. As a result, for a time, I was always off balance, physically and mentally.

As I was thinking back on this, a giggling feeling started from a deep part of me—from some place out in the universe. It reminded me that I should be extremely grateful I was not able to erase my self-awareness and spiritual knowing.

Still giggling, I walked out from the bedroom of our motor home. I explained to Robert how much Mama showed me. I said it was almost like a movie where a ghost takes you back to look at your life. The next day I went back to visit my mama's grave. I stopped again at the old farm and my beloved levee. It was October, and the wind was blowing cold. I stayed in my car for a short time, deciding to grab my blanket and head toward the levee. I made it halfway up the levee when my shoes became heavy with mud, and the cold wind was painful. I said to myself, "Bad idea—go back to your car." On my way back down, I slipped and fell on my behind, sliding all the way down to the road. I said out loud, "Good job, Maria," and laughed at how silly it felt to have a wet, muddy butt.

I could not get all the mud off my behind, so I put the blanket on my car seat and made the decision to go back to the motor home. In the meantime, I stayed in the car to warm up, so it was not long before I was again transported back in time.

The sun was warm while my car heated up. I started humming and lightly singing, "I am one with the light of the universe; I am light-filled." I was so comfortable, so relaxed, that I closed my eyes. I decided take a deep breath. It felt so good that I turned my car off and continued breathing in to the count of five, holding for five, and breathing out to the count of eight. I kept this up for about five minutes, relaxing, and without thought, I dropped my grounding cord to the center of earth. I visualized going to my special place deep within earth.

In this place, crystals lined my walls with water running out from my underground cave to the deepest depths of the ocean and earth. Then I said in a soft, loving voice, "I am centered and poised in the light of God." There was no effort going into my meditation. I thought of it, and it happened that fast. In the beginning, meditation seemed impossible to accomplish.

It was not always so easy for me to relax and clear my mind. I read many books on how to mediate and how to be psychic. The first time I walked into a bookstore it was so big I did not know how to find the books I wanted. I asked where I could find books on the occult and received that familiar look of disapproval. The man behind the counter pointed his finger. I took a deep breath and put my head down, but I went down row after row until I found the books. I was surprised there were so many to choose from; that day, I fell in love with bookstores. I could hear myself say, "It is all right, Maria. You can do this, so do not pay attention to the man."

I wanted to learn how to mediate but I not know how to achieve what I was looking. I began looking in the yellow pages for classes, schools, groups, or anybody who could help me understand and learn how to get back what I had hidden so well. In one of my adventures at a psychic fair, I picked up a flyer for a place called The Church of Enthusiasm and Joy founded by Jeff Serkin that advertised a class that fit my needs. The universe heard my prayer and sent me to the perfect place I needed.

The class always started with guided mediations, and the new kids on the block like me were given homework called affirmations. I was extremely excited with my newfound place to learn and have all my questions answered by people of great insight and wisdom.

My best discovery was that what they were teaching validated the fact that what I had known as a child was all true. The more classes I took, the bigger the validation became. This was one of the happy moments of my life in 1992

Through meditation and affirmations, I learned how to undo all the programming I had accepted growing up. I found a gateway to peace and quiet. Here, I found I could hear my soul's voice and clear my mind of daily chatter. Through the years, I have tried many different forms of meditation. I found that the one where I am grounded to earth and can run my energy works best for me. The reason I choose to drop my cord to the center of the earth is so that everything I release will not be sent out into the universe to manifest.

I release frustration, anger, worry, and many other negative emotions to the center of the earth to be neutralized, knowing that I have no fear that those thoughts can come back to me or someone else. I think of a boomerang-of-energy is a course of action that can backfire against its originator if something gets in its way. Remember, we are energy beings sending and receiving energy all the time. Sending thoughts to create thoughts that become a part of our lives in some form is called manifesting.

Learning how to mediate on my own was a challenge for a long time. It worked well in class, and I was determined to be able to do this on my own. After two years of studying, I learned how to meditate, what chakras were, and how to use this information to clean my mind and space to be free of anyone else's energy around me.

In the beginning, I read affirmations over and over until I memorized them, and when I needed help with overwhelming emotional pain or when I felt lost, I would use my affirmations. My favorite one was, "Today I am grateful, happy, healthy, and wealthy." I would repeat it over and over, and with time I only experienced wholeness along with my rediscovered wisdom. Yes, from time to time I still feel sadness or face difficult days, but I no longer stay in the negative place of thinking that I cannot find an answer.

Emotions are only temporary, and you will be shown how to resolve what is in front of you. Just sit still, take a few deep breaths, and hear the answer to your problem and how to handle it.

This is how I accomplished my foundation on meditation, chakras, auras, and grounding. Learning how to do these simple things gave me all the tools I needed to become a great psychic medium and healer while manifesting and being whole. I validate that part of all life and feel I am all with one.

I learned to manifest anything I wanted just by knowing it was mine to have without a doubt. My prayer was given to me when the universe said I should have it. I always give thanks ahead, knowing my wish has already happened. I wait with excitement and complete trust for my gift to arrive. In the beginning, I did not completely believe or trust that it would happen. As a result, I could not manifest anything, no matter how hard I wanted to.

Never ask to manifest anything when feeling anger, greed, or dishonesty against another soul. When you go into fear, you only create dysfunction, illness, stress, and discord.

Make a space for yourself and make it just your space. Once I found my perfect chair, I made sure there would not be any interference from the outside world, such as phones or television.

The minute I sat in my chair with the intent to meditate, it became my sanctuary. In the beginning, I tried burning incense or a good scented candle, and sometimes I had a small water fountain accompanied with soft music, but, in the end, all those things did not work. I chose quiet.

I learned to quiet my mind, to stop that record that plays all the time, and to stop thoughts that demand attention. Just like in my class, I closed my eyes, took three deep breaths through my nose, and slowly let the air out through my mouth. Then I sat back and relaxed my back, neck, shoulders, and jaw, letting the tension out. I placed my feet flat on the floor and my hands with my palms up on my lap. I moved around until my body was comfortable and completely free of tension. Now that I was comfortable, I kept my eyes closed and visualized looking at my aura and my seven major energy centers.

There are chakras in the middle of your feet, hands, and at the root that is the tip of the tail bone, also known as the sacrum. This area is where I attach my grounding cord. The reason for the cord is to create a pathway for all the negative energy to travel to the center of the earth and be diffused.

The first chakra is located across the pelvis where the pubic hair line starts forward to a portion of the hipbone. The second is at the navel. The third is at the solar plexus right under the heart. The fourth is the heart. The fifth is the throat. The sixth is the forehead. The seventh is the crown above the head, as are the eighth through tenth.

In my mind, I personally created chakras to look like daisies with a large, wide, round middle. I have friends who have created chakras to look like discs, a vortex, or a round cylinder. That is a personal choice that best fits a person. I made mine fun, which made it easier for me.

As I took a deep breath and centered myself, I allowed earth energy to flow up through the bottom of my feet. I opened the chakras under my feet just by thinking they were open, and I started receiving warm energy. Within seconds, I was enjoying the warm comfort of this encompassing energy under my feet, feeling its powerful energy lap around my toes and the sides of my feet. It felt as if I were soaking my feet in warm water. The earth's energy continued traveling and moving over my feet and up over my legs. I kept this warm energy moving up over my knees to my hips and over my stomach, heart, and head, enveloping each of the seven major chakras and then traveling back down my grounding cord and taking all the energy that was not for my highest good down my cord. I practiced this for several years before it was second nature.

In the beginning, I pictured the root of a tree, and finally I used a wide tube with a big basket at the end that I anchored into the earth.

I enjoyed cleaning my chakras and getting rid of the negative substances I had collected during my day. Each chakra has a different purpose in our bodies and souls, both physical and emotional.

I had fun cleaning my chakras. I would pretend I had this huge hose, somewhat like firemen use; I would spray each chakra, and it would tickle me. I would laugh so hard, and it felt great. I could see all the junk falling away down the ground cord—even faces and pain of things past.

The first time I did this exercise in class I was so amazed that I floated for days. I wore out my chakra hand out from class and made extra copies for myself.

In a few seconds in my mind's eye, I can still see the chakra paper in front of me even after so many years. I asked, "Mama, do you want to hear how well I memorized my chakras?"

She answered with a big, "Yes, let me hear it."

I smiled and yelled, "All right, I will say them out loud." I was feeling so proud and happy to have my mama next to me. I cleared my voice, and I sat up straight and started.

An Introduction to the Seven Chakras

First is the root chakra, earth, reproductive organs, and the lower limbs.

Positive Expression: purity, hope, joy, self-discipline, integration, perfection, wholeness, and nurturing

Unbalanced Expression: discouragement, hopelessness, impurity, and chaos

Second is below the navel, the sacral chakra, represented by water, sexual energy, and kidneys. It enhances drainage of waste from the lymphatic system.

Positive Expression: freedom, mercy, forgiveness, injustice, transcendence alchemy, transmutation diplomacy, intuition, prophecy, and revelation

Unbalanced Expression: lack of forgiveness, justice, mercy, intolerance, lack of tact, disregard for others, and cruelty

Third is the navel and solar plexus, considered fire, personal power and the body's energy center that directs healing. It is the body's storage of the life force, the lungs, which can be strengthened by deep breathing.

Positive Expression: peace, brotherhood, selfless service, right desire, balance, and harmlessness

Unbalanced Expression: anger, agitation, fanaticism, aggression, egoism, overindulgence, fear, anxiety, and passivity

Fourth is the heart center of the chest. Also to the right and left of the chest is called the secret heart, which governs the feminine and masculine receptivity.

Positive Expression: love, compassion, beauty, selflessness, sensitivity, appreciation, comfort, creativity, charity, and generosity

Unbalanced Expression: hatred, dislike, selfishness, self-pity, human sympathy, and negligence

Fifth is the throat that governs communication of knowledge, wisdom, emotional expression, connection, relationship, and spirit vibration.

Positive Expression: willpower, faith, protection, direction, courage, and obedience

Unbalanced Expression: control, condemnation, idle chatter, gossip, human willfulness, impotence, cowardice, and doubt

Sixth is located at the brow and shelters the senses, intuition, telepathy, meditation, and the portion of the brain that triggers relaxation, also known as the crown chakra of intuition and spirituality.

Positive Expression: illumination, wisdom, self-knowledge, understanding, humility, cosmic consciousness, and open-mindedness, intuition, and clarity

Unbalanced Expression: intellectual and spiritual pride, vanity, intellectualism, ego centeredness, narrow-mindedness, lack of vision, and criticism

Seventh is pure cosmic consciousness; intuition opens the crown chakra to the universe with enlightenment, containing the flowing life force of wholeness with insight, perception, psychic ability, wisdom, and clarity. It is the connection with the world when we are able to know all is one.

Positive Expression: complete understanding that we are wholeness

Unbalanced Expression: intellectual and spiritual pride, vanity, intellectualism, ego centeredness, and narrow-mindedness

"What do you think?" I asked her.

She replied in a soft voice, "Very good, Maria. It sounds like that helped you a lot. Tell me more."

My reason for learning and understanding the function of my chakras was important to me so I could completely be in touch with my body, mind, and soul and understand my wholeness. Exploring my energy system helped me move toward self-discovery, and the practice of being in the present moment with a strong foundation helped me learn to trust completely.

Now I understand that within my heart live the power,

presence, and completeness of the universe. I choose to experience the greatness within; I let go of yesterday and any criticism I may have made upon myself. I release shame, guilt, and any negative thoughts I may have about myself. I now choose to love myself and accept my goodness. I am unique and special. I realize my strength and the limitless power within me.

Back in the present I said, "Sorry, Mama. My butt is still wet, and I have to leave soon. When out of the blue I was transferred in a flash back to how dreams started my path to classes. I was having a wonderful time remembering my teachers and classes. Alright I am back, let's finish our conversation."

I know I did not cause problems and it was in no way my fault when family or friends did not like me or did not like what I said or did. I do not take anything personally when I am talked about or people disagree with me. Everyone is part of me. They are entitled to their way of thinking and will find their place. I do not judge.

It did take me several years in the beginning to trust the answer I heard given to me. Trusting my message, my intuition, and the voice of my inner soul took me time. The classes helped, but it was up to me to do the work.

I was born with the ability to be a psychic medium and healer. That never disappeared; I had just buried it deep within my unconscious. Once I pulled it back up, it came easily. I just had to trust again what I would hear. Being validated was quick and wonderful; I love myself and enjoy the knowledge of being part of the whole universe.

Intuition is born with us. Some have more than others, and some just do not want it, just as I did not when I was young and tried to bury it. This I know of intuition. It is important to use it when it presents itself as an extrasensory perception of

knowledge, such as the telepathic awareness of something another person is thinking, clairvoyance (knowledge of a physical
happening), precognition (predicting a future event), or being
sensitive to all the clues such as the ability to see auras and
chakras with color or on a knowing level with color. This all
fuses into a level of knowing.

Knowing is possessing knowledge on any subject, idea, or
problem with intelligence and comprehension. In an instant,
when your mind is searching for an answer, you have comprehension and exhibit clever awareness and resourcefulness. It is
your gut feeling. Once I understood how to harness all the information within, I was proud to be a psychic or a sensitive—a
word used by many.

An enormous step for me was recognizing the universe as
a living presence of goodness, truth, beauty, peace, power, and
love. I understand that its energy is alive and connects all living
things and that everything is energy in different forms. This is
how I reconnected with my higher, innermost self in the form
of ideas filled with information. Usually I receive what I truly
need at that moment. I connect dreams and intuition by trusting and returning to dreams and listening to my fears about
what I did not want to know, even if Mama's voice was over-
riding my voice.

I jumped with joy and laughed so long my voice was sore
with happiness when I realized I had finally figured it out.

"Mama," I said, "let me take you back to my dreams and
what I learned about trusting my intuition and accepting my
ability to read psychic perceptions."

Once I understood that my dreams were messages from my
own self, it was easier to find help with understanding my fears
and how I was hiding my fears unconsciously. I had blocked

many hurts alongside the happiness so I could function daily, but dreams did not let me forget what the problem was.

I spent three years of studying Earnest Homes and many others who covered a wealth of spiritual knowledge. He was just one of many authors and different teachers at Church of Enthusiasm and Joy.

Each class was designed to cover subjects step by step on relationships, anger management, couples therapy, grief counseling, human behavior, personality disorders, love, self-esteem, spiritual growth, and learning how to trust ourselves first and then to trust others.

Trust was, and at times still is, my highest mountain to reach. I have struggled with trust most of my life. I was criticized about everything; therefore, I did not trust who I was. After my husband cheated on me, I no longer trusted him. Once I suffered being violated, I did not trust anyone. I decided to work on confidence first. My integrity and good character was intact.

In spite of the problem I had with my father, I am grateful to him for instilling in me the importance of being honest, truthful, and knowing that my word had to be as good as gold. I always kept all promises, and I respect integrity. This is my foundation, so I began my quest to find confidence in myself, my identity, and what I wanted in life.

It took me years to completely have confidence and trust in myself. Talking to my mama helped me know it was not my burden to carry because of her fears. She thought she was protecting me—that being normal and doing as I was told would keep me safe.

Once I accepted that I was psychic and that was my normal, I trusted the difference between visions that came from within to show me how to navigate the realms of thought, feeling, and emotion, but it took a lot of practice. Also, navigating what I see with my actual eyes and what I see with my spiritual eyes was difficult because the two sights were completely opposite. I came to depend on my spiritual eyes for truth.

After three years of study, loving myself appeared along with trusting myself, having confidence in myself, and realizing my psychic ability.

My inner source revealed that when life begins with the first breath at birth, our souls' breath also begins, and our universal source of information comes with us. All I did was be still and listen, and answers were revealed in different forms of the intuition. Dreams were first to remind me that I am an energetic being from an intelligent, spiritual source of energy and that the universe expresses its love through me.

Life is light energy, and my light shines through my body with a great array of color. This bright energy light moves faster than the speed of light. In fact, light and time is everywhere at the same time. *Energy* is a clumsy word. It does not denote how alive the body is and how trillions of cells can cooperate to create a whole. My soul's voice comes from that light. I increased my positive energy and became incredibly brighter and more alive.

Another facet of intuition is a direct form of knowing that bypasses the normal, rational process of thinking. It comes from a higher plain of information that comes with us.

I could hear Mama calling me and asking why I did not make it to visit her at the grave site. I responded, "Sorry. I stopped at our old house, went up the levee, and got wet and muddy, so I turned around and came to the motor home. I will be there tomorrow. I also wanted to visit my giant and feel his presence again. I know I can visualize him, but it is always better for me to be there. Good night, Mama. I will see you tomorrow. I also need to talk to you. Thank you for contacting me."

She answered, "Maria, believe me when I tell you I was always with you and helping you during your learning. Did you think you found The Church of Enthusiasm and Joy all by yourself? I am sorry I did not make it easy for you when I was here on earth. I also was not schooled in many ways and was filled with fear of spirits and intuition. I did not know how to help you when you were afraid, and you did not know it was all right to be mad as hell and scream it out, so you repressed your emotions. Now please do not forget what I requested from you the first day you came to see me."

"Mama, I always keep my word," I promised her.

CHAPTER 5

Learning to Use My Intuition

After visiting with my mama, I was grateful for her time and conversation. I was feeling proud of my journey and feeling a deep satisfaction knowing that she was always with me, smiling; I could feel her warmth hugging me.

My bedroom was cool, so on my way to turn the heater on I opened my blinds to see what the weather was like. To my surprise, it was lightly raining, and a cool wind was blowing. I felt a shudder of fear knowing I had to drive to Woodland. As the motor home warmed up, I made myself some coffee and sat with a blanket over me as I watched the miracle of rain and wind moving the trees from side to side along the fence.

The steam from my coffee smelled so good, and it was so hot and delicious that with a couple of deep breaths I was in a meditational state. Robert and my animals were sound asleep, so I was at peace playing in the universe and checking in to see how family and friends were doing.

In the stillness of my morning, I called Mama and invited her to sit with me on my warm, cozy couch. It had taken me years to learn how to fully use all my psychic ability.

"Mama, I know you can hear me," I called.

"Yes, I can, Maria," she responded.

"It is so wonderful that I can see and hear you now," I continued. "Mama, can I tell you how I learned to use my intuition to help myself and others?"

"I would love that," she said.

I felt her sit next to me, and her presence filled my room with love and energy.

Exploring my intuition showed me my source is my soul. Source is the light in me and everyone. Once I began my journey of understanding the power of my intuition, it was a map to knowing what my soul is and what my purpose is.

I had fun seeing and reading auras in class; once again, I was validated. I would do a little jig with my arm high in the sky full of satisfaction, that I first saw auras when I was little girl around five or six. I just did not know what I was seeing, so I thought that everybody saw them.

When pupils had a difficult time seeing an aura in class, they were given a book that allowed them to see a three-dimensional picture when they stared into an image on the page. That would help train the eye to see an aura. Sometimes the class went outdoors to look at the leaves on trees and watch the auras move with the leaves. It was very cool to train the eye to see outside the box of ordinary sight.

An aura is energy that surrounds all living things. Humans have seven layers in their auras, the same as chakras. Color around a person reflects the physical, mental, emotional, and spiritual state. Chakras can also vibrate with the same colors.

A deep or vibrant aura is usually a person who is confident, strong, assertive, and extroverted and who, at times, can be stubborn or overpowering. A person who works or plays hard may need to rest or relax more.

A pale or soft color is usually a person who is sensitive, gentle, and introverted and has a tendency to allow others to step on him. This type of energy in a person is one who is a healer or psychic. These people need to control their energy properly by guarding their energy field, so that they do not become drained by others.

A dark, black, or even sometimes colorless or white aura is fear or illness. It can mean that we are hiding or that we wish to keep private from the world, so we pull our energy or aura in closer to our physical bodies like armor.

A large aura that covers most of the body is a person who is putting out a lot of angry energy in front of themselves. You can usually feel that person coming before you see them.

Chakras, auras, emotions, and memories are all energy centers full of information to help us understand why we are in pain or why we are in happy, blissful places.

Learning to tap into that information comes with time and results from an interest in wanting to make a different choice of how to live happily and be whole. To love ourselves and forgive ourselves for old wrongs is where we start. I see auras and chakras as small rivers that lead to important truths of who we are.

As children we know we are energy beings—part of the larger whole—and we see and hear spirits. Many children like me learn to be fearful of rejection, and because we run the risk being called crazy, we hide our internal innocence and knowledge.

Not just myself, but all human beings, possess psychic ability with different characteristics. By understanding my energy system, I was able to find which was the strongest for me. All senses, both physical and psychic, are constantly receiving and responding to some form of energy or stimuli; I was unconsciously accessing my sixth sense all the time. I was simply not aware of all the elements of my own intuition. Some people, such as my friend Patsy, are empathic. She often felt overwhelmed by everybody's emotions. She would become physically ill and take on the symptoms of whomever she had sympathy for. Psychic empathy's are sensitive, and they easily pick up negative energy and magnify it, taking and making the emotions of others their own emotions. Like so many empathy's, she was usually late for work and even for her personal appointments. Patsy would get so caught up in holding a person's hand or hugging someone and listening to him when he was in need that she would lose track of time. In return, she expected sympathy and attention for her kindness.

Dress code is a problem for empathic people; they like to dress casually and comfortably, so business clothing is difficult for them.

Patsy would make important decisions based on feeling instead of being practical or analyzing a situation. If it did not feel right, you could not move her. She is a great friend and the most loving woman I know, so it was hard to see her become ill, especially when her stomach and lower back would hurt. She could not understand why. I kept telling her how to survive and thrive. All she had to do was learn how to separate her own emotions and physical being from the pain of others. Because recognizing the problem is half the solution, once she knew why she became sick, she could see what negative ideas controlled her life and overwhelmed her sensory awareness.

I was on a mission to find which psychic ability was my most dominant. All I knew in the beginning was that everyone has abilities, but we each have one that is greater. We have several different intuitive gut feelings. I was on a quest to find my strongest.

I found it, and I was again validated when I realized I had known this when I was between five and seven. I am a psychic medium who can read and see with spiritual eyes and with a knowing, intuitive strength. It took me years to trust everything I heard and saw on a knowing level. Trust is the key.

A characteristic of a knowing, feeling person is that she is instantaneous. Many times when I was in a conversation, I knew before someone would finish the sentence what he was going to say. Ask me any question, and I could hear the answer in an instant. I am almost always on target. The only time I am not is if I run into someone who is holding his aura so tightly or has no sense of right or wrong in his being. I have no doubt what my messages are. I am connected to the whole universe and instantaneously know we are part of the collective whole.

Information comes to me in a fraction of time, but in a flash I receive premonitions or predictions. If asked a question quickly, I know the answer. I do not worry because I know everything will work out and how it will play out.

Once I was able to put my ego completely out of the way, I trusted myself and my strongest ability: knowing. My thoughts, ideas, and concepts, both conscious and unconscious, are the sum total manifested as my experience. I learn to understand all I have been and all I have done is based upon what I believed to be true.

My teacher drilled it into all her students: "Believe what you hear; trust the process." Each soul must take responsibility for its awakening. Each soul must choose. If you truly want to end your experience of separation, you must be sincere. The secret lies in knowing where and how to look. Everything starts with consciousness. Healthy energy is flowing, flexible, dynamic, and balanced in a positive feeling. This process leads you to know intuition that will help you have the insight to discover a way to start a conversation with yourself and determine who you were born to be.

I spoke to Mama again and she said, "Tell me more, Maria; I am enjoying your teachers and how they helped change many souls."

I had a lot of fun trying remote viewing of what was in my knowing area. I went into a complete deep mediation. I selected a remote location to scan. I asked myself what I sensed about it, if someone was there, and what was happening. Then I wrote down all my impressions and trusted all impressions of what I saw, heard, and smelled without censor. I allowed my hand to draw and write all the information I received. The more I practiced, the more precise I became.

"Now, Mama," I added, "let's move on to the psychic hearing reception area. It is important to be aware and pay special attention to the ears. This is important because your knowing is behind the eyes and around your ears. A clairaudient has an inner hearing often quite similar to what you hear in your mind when you are thinking or when you talk to yourself."

Hearing involves extrasensory signals, such as words or other forms of language, together with and inner, mental dialogue. People who receive their messages through their hearing are not satisfied completely until they understand they are clairaudient. They must be able to analyze and understand the messages they are receiving. Listening to all sounds that you can possibly hear is important because it will give you a reference to outside voices and sounds, as well as to your inner hearing. Practice sensing your ears and imagine them large and able to catch sound in the same way a cat's or dog's ears catch sounds.

When I wanted to hear, I would start by sitting in a long mediation late at night. I would ask my higher being to separate me from my exterior world. In this place, I have the power of hearing and mental telepathy. It took me a lot of practice to hear my inner voice clearly. Keeping my mind clear of false notions was not an easy task; it required me to know my own and others' beliefs. To achieve total silence in my mind took me a long time.

At first I would write down all words I heard without judging until I knew the difference between my thinking messages. Sending and receiving words is fun and amazing.

In the same general area above the eyebrow area is the location for vision via psychic sight. Visionaries need to see things both physically and through mental images. Metaphysics call the forehead the third eye region, and many religions anoint or decorate the forehead in baptismal or other blessing rituals. Visionaries see messages in many formats, such as billboards, newspapers, ads, and books. It all starts with a quiet mind so you can focus on the area where your strengths are.

When I tried to discover my abilities, I would go into mediation and ask the universe which one of the six senses was my strongest. I received my answer and concentrated on the area of my knowing and where on my physical body I was going to feel it. There it was. I felt a pang, pain, numbness, and my stomach became upset. With time, I learned to distinguish which pain or discomfort I was feeling, on what intensity level I was feeling it, and what part of my body I needed to intuitively look at.

I also learned to know where the pain would settle when anger of past hurts would come up. I would continue my meditation to release anger and forgive myself and the person who hurt me. Again, down the grounding cord they went.

Forgiving was not easy for me in the beginning, but the ability to forgive allowed me to learn the value of the ultimate healing force of love. I could heal myself and learn how to love myself.

Horrible things had happen to me, and somehow I believed it was my fault—that I created the problem. Even to this day, as I write this book, hurtful memories pop up to show me the value of those who hurt me.

They were great teachers. They showed me how to forgive myself and others, how to not feel guilty about my bad choices, and how to love my strengths and the perfect woman I am. In short, they showed me that I am free to be me.

I finished my dialogue and said, "Mama, I am finished for today. Thank you for sitting next to me and allowing me to chew your ear off."

My mama laughed loudly, and I remembered her wonderful voice from my childhood. "Maria," she said, "you are as silly as ever."

I answered, "I know. I love being funny and happy."

I started my car, backed out onto the road, and was on my way to Cal Expo to my motor home—my home away from home. I was still feeling grateful and delighted, so I turned on the radio and started singing and yelling, "Thank you, Universe." Love swept through me, uplifting me and making me realizing I am happy to know that my psychic abilities gave me back my identity. I yelled out the car window. "Thank you, Mama, for showing old memories."

It's amazing how having back my identity empowered me. My first husband beat, tortured, belittled me, and caused me to feel terrified for years of my life and my children's lives. His terror included his gun, and his favorite game was playing Russian roulette with me. My second husband would slap me around to control me. It was my fault I got hit. If only I would do as I was told, he would not get angry. At this time I was struggling for a voice in second marriage. I had enrolled in college and took criminal justice. I wanted to understand law enforcement and hoped to understand my second husband.

I was under a lot of stress to both find myself and stay married. I would tell myself that it was just stress and that I would be fine, but I was in way over my head. Not knowing what my body and mind were feeling, I looked up the meaning of the word *stress* in the dictionary. It means a hardship or an applied force or system that tends to strain or deform the body through mental, emotional, or physical tension, strain, or distress. When taken to a further extreme, look at the definition of distress: to cause anxiety or suffering, to worry. The following semester I took a psychology class to find out how and why I was trapped in a situation of anger that took such control of my emotions that I lost objectivity. I did not understand what stress—or anger—really was.

Conflict became an unavoidable part of my daily life. I came to believe my second husband was right, and I was in the wrong when he said that I should consider myself lucky he married me with children and all. Conflict became an unavoidable part of my life because my beliefs, or lack of my own belief system, often contrasted powerfully. Once I understood that I could choose to think differently, I worked on becoming whole and peaceful.

"Oh, Mama," I exclaimed, "To be aware and alive in the eternal light of divinity makes me humble and grateful. I remember back when I was lost in an abyss of rage, and I reacted instead of feeling grateful for my life."

I was looking to draw in a breath of fresh air that could relieve the ache in my heart. I could not see anything or anyone else in front of me because my emotional pain blinded me to anything else.

I wanted more than anything to save my marriage, but I could not even save myself. It would take me nine years after that divorce from James my second husband and a lot of studying for me to be able to put one foot in front of the other. I discovered how to have self-esteem, love, and appreciation for myself; I, Maria Garay, emerged.

Spiritual practice does not place your focus on your personal need. A rule, or principle, of the soul is that while knowing all things and doing all things, it is source that brings absolute freedom. To the soul there is no work to be done. Everything we want is already ours. Yet all work is done by the presence of the soul. The soul, as it is called, is the divine "I am" in each man, woman, and child. Recalling and doing my spiritual work and practicing meditation to regain my intuition were my baby steps into changing my life.

Now I am in my car going home, my music is on, and I am singing and loving my wonderful, amazing life.

CHAPTER 6

Medium

My dialogue with my mama continued after I reached my motor home. I spoke to her and said, "Mama, the first day I was at your grave site, you told me that there are many souls waiting to talk to loved ones. You also mentioned that each soul chooses the medium it wants to send its message to loved ones with. Tell me more. I was so excited to speak with you that I do not remember every detail you told me about being a medium."

Mama responded, "Come sit down. Close your eyes and go into mediation. Take a deep breath in, hold it, and let your breath out slowly. Go to your special room in the center of your creative mind. I want you to run your energy from the bottom of your feet, over your head, and all the way back to your feet. I do not want you to ground to the middle of earth and send unwanted energy there. The center of the earth is not a place to dump unwanted thoughts and fears. Instead, I want you to take the earth's healing and dissolve those feelings into the nothingness where it came from. This will purify your thoughts, body, mind, and soul. By releasing ideas, your aura and chakras will be cleansed.

"I have heard about all your advances and the healing work you have done when you were stuck and lost your identity. You have had great teachers. I am proud you went back to the intuition that led you back to me. By knowing all life is one big DNA and that everything on this earth is connected to source, you discovered you are source.

"I have been with you and tried to guide you to a good, positive direction. Do you remember when you would pass by a bookstore and have to go in?"

I thought about what she said and responded. "Now that you mention it, I do remember that I always felt a big pull and would go in a positive direction without really knowing why. I always bought a book that gave me answers I needed.

"So, Mama," I said, "tell me why you want me to be a medium."

She replied, "I do not want you to be a medium; you are already one.

"When you were little, I am sorry I did not take the time to explain that there is a bad entity that can cause problems. There are also demons, as you learned in your studies. I also know that is why you had not used your medium ability. I did not intend to create fear for you. This is the reason I called you to visit me. I needed to have this conversation about you being a medium, and you must understand the importance of this request."

"Maria, you know that everything is connected and that nothing dies. Energy beings exist everywhere the energy of human beings and the energy of other spiritual beings is. All these beings exist here on earth.

"Let me take you back to when you chose me and your father for parents. Remember, you picked us."

"Yes, Mama," I said, "you are right, but how do you know

this? There is no separation of being alive or dead. People are just blind to what their eyes have been trained to see."

She explained, "As a sensitive person, you can see and hear all beings, because you went back to your ability of being connected to earth and your source. Your source has no limits.

"Let's get back to what I said the first day at Woodland Cemetery. First, I said there are energy beings that no longer have a human body and that they need to talk to loved ones. They choose the medium they think will give the message correctly. Not all mediums give the message word by word; some make something up that is not true. I know you have been contracted by spirits in the past few months, and they relayed to me that you gave the message correctly.

"Next, I said spirits only come in on their own terms. So if you have a room full of people wanting to hear from a loved one, and no spirit shows up to tell the people why and how their loved ones did not show, it is unfortunate. They may just need a reading or healing. That will be up to you remember to see, know, and feel—all because you are source.

"Finally Meditate. Before you receive a guest looking to connect with spirits, clean your room with sage or with incense. Ask source to guide you and be grateful for the opportunity to be of service. Ask all lower spirits to leave the room, because your light shines bright and they may try to come in. When spirits come to you to help them be free from being bound to the earth, help them.

They do not go into the light, but they are free to move to all reaches of the universe. They will not haunt a place because their spirits can go play. I have seen you help children find their way. They loved your bright light and knew you would help them. I personally thank you for that.

"It will not take you practice, because you were born a psychic with high abilities. I just scared you, and for that I am sorry. Now that you know what you are, all your fears should be gone forever.

"I want you to do the same for the souls that need to connect, to feel free, and to play happy. If a loved one holds them here because she still has sorrow about their transition, you need to help them let them go.

"I have seen how much you have loved and still love all beings. The orbs love you. Be grateful for their insight, and they will continue to help you. I am so glad that when you heard them you paid attention and became a friend. If you need more help being a medium, just call me."

CHAPTER 7

Orbs from Brazil

*A*gain I needed to communicate with my mama. I said, "Mama, hello I need to talk to you. Could you please come and visit with me now?" I waited for a long time and called out to her again. "Woodland is so far, and I would like to talk to about orbs. I made discoveries when I went to Brazil to see John of God the healer. I will come visit you tomorrow as I promised, but I was so excited about my trip that I forgot to share it with you.

"I will start my conversation, and you can jump in anytime you like. I was deep in the Brazilian jungle, climbing up the side of a mountain to reach the top of the beautiful waterfalls. I sat down to rest, and the mist of the water felt good and cooled me off after I was huffing and puffing on the steep mountain.

"I looked out and saw this bright blue butterfly. Beside it was a round sphere and what appeared to be a tall man dressed in a long white robe. The group of friends I was with passed me up and rushed ahead to reach the top of the waterfall. I heard my inner voice telling me to stay behind and listen. I told the group I would stay behind with my sketchpad and camera.

"I was in awe of the bright blue butterflies all around me and the different colored balls. I heard a distant voice and waited to hear where it was coming from. I turned around, looking to see if anyone was behind me, but I did not see anyone, so I called, 'Hello, anybody there?' I waited for an answer but did not receive a response.

"I located the perfect flat, dry place to sit and catch my breath so I could start my sketching. To my amazement, as I was admiring the waterfall, I saw a transparent ball that appeared again next to a rainbow created by the waterfall. My first thought was that it was created by the water mist. Pure magic was all around me, so I settled down on my perfect flat rock and just sat quietly, filling my heart with love and happiness.

"Out of the corner of my eye, I saw the tall man again. He seemed to be floating beside the small waterfall. He was wearing a long white robe, and his long hair and beard ran together. The white robe covered his feet. I could see the blue butterflies through him and more round, clear orbs.

"I took a deep breath and was so overwhelmed by the sweeping greatness that I wept with happiness. At that moment, I remembered life is one of living in the moment. From the time everyone is born, you come into this world with the understanding that every minute you take a breath you are connected to all life.

"I was back on my giant's eyebrow, and even the man who came to visit me when I was a small child was there. This experience erased any doubt that my giant was exactly as I remembered him to be. There I was on my giant's eyebrow, soul diving in Brazil just like at home on the Sacramento levee."

"Mama, did you hear me calling you from Brazil?" I asked. "I also yelled as loudly as I could, 'I am Maria from Elkhorn Ferry, one with the universe. Look at me here. I am in the rain forest of Brazil.'"

My journey to La Casa De Dom Inacio De Layola to see John of God, Joao de Deus, was indescribable. People from all corners of the world, poor and rich, go to see Joao, looking and hoping to find a cure for whatever illness. All people who go before John of God dress in white clothes. Some days all you see is a mass of white clothes for as far as the eye can see. I personally visited him three different years, and I have witnessed and felt his healing power. I have seen this man do surgery, dig out horrible-looking things with only his fingers. I cannot describe the healing that takes place on both a mental and physical level.

I was teaching intuitive healing in Placerville, California, at that time. As a class group, we all went to Brazil with a travel guide, Catherina Haines. She was an angel. Without her, my personal experience would not be so great away from the casa visiting other cities and healers. She took us on a tour of Brazil away from the tourist places. The heart of Brazil, which she showed us, was magnificent and magical. I was able to experience healers, earth, music, exceptional food, juices, and beautiful, friendly people. All my senses went on overload, and when I close my eyes, I can still see and smell them all.

Native Indians from the jungle came down to Abadiania, Brazil, a small village where the casa is located. I met many people from all parts of the world with different stories, all looking to be healed.

In this small village at the edge of town is where it was my honor to meet a medicine man called Jaguar. Even at this very moment I have no words to describe this extraordinary man other than he is a beautiful, wild part of the universe and has great healing power.

When our eyes met, I looked directly into source, and when he put his hand over my heart, the connection was instant. He told me I had a good heart, that I was his mother, and that he loved me as much. I felt his energy flow through my entire soul, and in that instant, we were completely connected forever. Jaguar is the shaman of his tribe. The only word he said to me in English was "Mother" as he placed his hand on his heart and back to mine.

Four of us were invited to have lunch the next day at Jaguar's family's house. We sat on the floor, and the food was served on a matt in front of us. They gave each of us a bowl and a spoon. They served fish soup and lots of fresh fruit. The food was tasty and different.

I have never had fish soup in my life, so it was new to me. I felt loved and blessed with kindness. They did not speak English, but language is not always necessary. I played with the kids, laughed a lot, and had a great time. Abadiania was filled with miracles every day at the casa and the village as a whole.

The airplane trip was long and sleepless. As we landed I was so tired, but looking at this great country woke me up. The city was surrounded by jungle. The buildings were plain but colorful, and even the tallest hotel had all the windows open.

I walked toward our bus. It was not what I expected a bus to look like. To me it looked more like an old van. The driver was polite with a wide smile. His face was dark from the sun, and the wrinkles around his eyes made his green eyes appear brighter. He was a good-looking man.

On the way to the casa, Cat told us some of the rules and the dos and don'ts at the casa. We were told all guests had to wear white clothes before we were to appear before John of God. We were told to write down our illness or whatever reason we were there for and give it to the translator.

Anticipation ran wild in me as I was waiting in line to talk with John of God. If he invited you to sit in the current room meditating next to him, I was told you had to keep your eyes closed and not cross your legs or arms. I was told if I crossed my hands or feet, the flow of energy would stop.

It was finally my turn, and I did not know if I should stand or kneel in front of him. As his translator handed him my note, and before I decided what to do, he made a gesture for me to kneel. He put his hand on top of my head, and the rush of his high energy was so hot that I fell to the floor. I felt his staff pick me up and put me in a room with caretakers to tend to me. Cat came in to the recovery room, helped me up, gave me coconut milk, and helped me to my room. I stayed in bed for two days while food from the kitchen was brought in for me. The instant that he touched my head, I purged years of agony I was holding onto on an unconscious level deep in my soul.

That purging was the beginning of my book *Autopsy of a Soul*. The next time I went up before John of God, I asked if I should write this book. He took my hand and said, "Yes," and told me that I would write other books and that I would help many. He laid his hand on the notebook I was carrying, and that was the beginning of my becoming an author.

It was Friday and our last day when he handed me two large crystals—one male and one female. His translator explained the male and female had to be centered and in balance.

John of God told me to meditate with them and to keep them only to myself. He said they would help me on my writing journey. When I needed healing or information, I was to hold my crystals and trust the answer. His translator told me that I must soak them in salt water once a month to keep them clean and to never let anybody else see or touch them.

I thought I had released all that pain from the past, but

it turned out that I still had lingering deep emotional post-traumatic stress within, at an extremely deep place in my soul. John of God healed me on many levels. As I started to write my book, I knew why the book had to be written. He healed and cleared problems I did not know I had. He is an amazing man who knew what was wrong with me.

It would be four years after that journey before I would see orbs again with my eyes and take pictures of their faces with my camera.

Orbs are high-frequency energy beings that come in many colors and shapes. I later remembered when I was informed at a shaman's gathering in Brazil that I would be blessed to be connected with the universe, and orbs would be appearing to say hello or give me a message when the time was right.

I was taking pictures late one night, and I asked, "What do you want with me?"

I heard a soft whisper, almost too light to hear. "We are here to protect and guide you. Now take a breath and remember when you were young and you saw a huge orange sphere hovering over you. It pulsated and had a distinct color that would deepen in intensity. The next day you asked your father what it was, and he said it was a lightning ball."

When I returned home from Brazil, we moved to Deming, New Mexico, and I did not think much about orbs. I was busy packing and preparing our house in Pollock Pines, California, to go on the market. The house sold quickly, and the house we wanted in New Mexico was perfect. At that time I thought it was meant to be, because it happened so fast and with no effort. My husband had wanted to move to New Mexico for many years, but I had been reluctant to move so far because all my children lived in California. I had mixed feelings, but Robert was so happy and it all happened so fast—with no effort. I thought it was to be my new path. Here, in the middle of the desert, I found orbs again.

Orbs are considered to be entities, energy, spirits, angels, ascended masters, or even ancestors. They are here to remind us of other dimensions around everyone that human eyes and ears cannot see or hear. They are here to remind us we are more than just living creatures we call humans. We are orbs with bodies. All humans possess their own individual surrounding aura and energy. That aura space is made up of the body of the universe, and our physical bodies are concentrated spaces we can tap into, loaded with information when we want it. When we want to manifest anything in our lives, this energy goes out to the universe like orbs and comes back with the answer or wish.

We can tap into that information and look at the world with our spiritual eyes and call on the orbs as emissaries of our higher selves for answers. From this space, we can use our intuition and channel our higher self-knowing.

Orbs can be called to appear, or they may appear when they want. Quiet your mind and call the orbs, and they will come. Ask your question, listen for answers, and trust what you hear. They know your spirit, and your bright energy will guide them to you.

They whispered to me that love is the face and body of the universe. It is the connective tissue of the universe—the stuff of which we are made. Love is the experience of being whole and connected to the universal divinity given to you at birth. It extends beyond anything we can imagine in that it is infinite, wrapping in and around us and every other living thing. It is us.

Colored orbs are caused by vibration, because the universe is an expression of visible and invisible pulsation of light energy.

Color varies from white, gold, blue, clear, and many other hues that are open to interpretation, but you can see faces in the orbs or in the formations they make. They can offer us a new perspective on spirituality by encouraging us to open our senses to new dimension of reality and preparing all of us for their touch and words of wisdom.

There is no death. Life just takes on different forms as the energy transfers from one vessel or embodiment to the next. An example is a tree becoming the lumber to build a home or paper for a book, but throughout the process, the item still contains the living essence of a tree.

Clouds are also a great source of energy for seeing angels and other large beings smiling down at us. Dragons and other fabulous animals often visit us from above and peek through the clouds. The mystery of the universe is at your fingertips; just ask to see, and all will appear. Only habitual thinking keeps humans chained to their present behaviors. The more sensitive we become and learn that we are beings of light and one with universe, the more we will see into other dimensions. Information is endless. Just look up or ask the universe and trust what you hear.

I was taking a bath when I heard voices talking outside my bathroom window. It was late, around ten o'clock at night, and I was getting ready for bed. I quickly put a towel over my hair and grabbed my robe. I called out to the orbs and asked if they were talking to me.

I heard one say, "Yes, it is us; I will talk for the rest of us."

I left my robe on and went outside with a chair and a blanket around me to keep warm. On the way out I grab my camera.

I said, "I am ready. I was in Brazil when I first saw your light and faces. What are you called, or do you have a special name?"

"I am Zoron, and I have been with you since you asked your father what that round ball in the sky was. His answer was a bolt of light. I have traveled with you since.

"I called you tonight to help you with the war between your emotions and intuition. Conflict within alters our emotions. Fear, hurt, the unknown, loneliness, jealousy, betrayal, and even envy of others cause our emotional adrenaline to run wild and control all our actions.

"Regardless of how hard you try to control your mind with logic or the fact that you know better, while you are in the state of emotional overdrive, it is impossible for you to find your center until you feel safe and gain control again. If you become stuck in fear too long, you can become paralyzed. Emotions will pass and release their grip. When you find yourself in these moments of acting out with no control, it is a great time to depend on your intuition to help see with clarity instead of being blinded by the adrenaline of survival.

"Start breathing; close your eyes and take a deep breath that fills your diaphragm. Hold it to the count of five and release it through your mouth with lips open. Do this at least three times. Maria, you know what you need to do to place yourself in the present moment and calm down."

I respond, "I know, but my husband is going to transition before long. I am not sure how to still my mind. As I start to quiet my mind, all I hear is that my husband only has 20 to 25 percent of his heart that works. I need to take him home to Sacramento or Placerville, so he can have the best doctor he needs."

They answered, "We know you want to go home and that your husband is ill, but you need to get centered. Remember, you can manifest what you want with your source power to call in the universe. Ask, and you shall receive.

"We are all here as your support system to help you with this difficult situation you face. Three of us will be with you from this point on until you move back home to California and your husband's transition. Leave California to us and start packing. Begin your house hunting and put your house up for sale."

We had moved to Deming, New Mexico, in 2005 because my husband, Robert, dreamed for years of living in the desert. Deming housing was affordable. I wanted to move below the snow line of Pollock Pines. Our home in Pollock Pines sold quickly, so to me that was a sign it was time to move, and New Mexico was far below the snow line.

I did not see in my forecast that one year later I was going to be homesick for my family and for California. This is when I began my journey to get back to California, and if that was not enough, my husband had become extremely sick.

Being a strong woman, I took pride in being able to stay centered, keep my emotions happy, and live in the moment. However, I would experience doubt, and meditation became difficult.

The second year in Deming is when my husband's heart problems first appeared. The visits in and out of the hospitals happened often, and I went into fear. The more doctors told me about my husband's short life span, the more I bought the idea they were correct. I lost my ability to center myself and stay focused. This had a short life span because I took back my knowledge that all was going to be good and blasted fear away with the light of source shining on me.

Again, from that deepest part of my soul, I cried out to the universe to get me home and help me get back. It would take us four years to get back home to Placerville and into the arms of my children, brothers, and all my beautiful friends.

Money problems changed overnight, and we bought a home. I gave thanks to Zoron and the orbs for letting me know I had a long, safe journey ahead of me.

CHAPTER 8

The Art of Practicing Soul Diving

Soul diving for me was discovering how to love myself and trust and believe in my abilities. It was the incredible power of tapping into my own self-worth and knowing and believing without a doubt that I was a whole energy being. I was the connective tissue—the source of the universe.

Diving into my source, that deepest part of my soul, was to retrieve not only buried unconscious and conscious information I stored but also to retrieve memories of an innocent time, as well as shame and cowardice. I felt proud, but I also felt many mixed emotions, both the highs and lows—each a great teacher. At times, I would hide information about me from myself. I could not hear what I said to myself, and when someone told me something about me that was not flattering, I would deny it was part of me. That slowed my progress down to a crawl.

It did not mean that I would never have a bad day or another sad day. I knew I would hear the answer to move on and find the positive answer out of a hard day. Knowing I had the power to change my day was my little piece of heaven.

I spoke again. "Mama, thank you for helping me back in time to fill in some memories I did not understand. I understand that your fear of demons visiting me or taking procession of my body was a possibility. Your fear is what scared me and made a big impact.

"The best way I can describe what I mean is that it created a rip on a soul level. I did not trust that something bad would not happen to me. For a long time I was scared of the dark, especially the dark closet without a door in your bedroom. I knew for sure a demon was going to get me. I even thought for sure a stranger would hurt me on my levee.

"During our conversation, I could feel again how I played in the rainbow and skipped to each of its colors. Each color is full of energy and singing. Talking with entities tickled me and was pleasurable. It is fun when energy beings join me in conversations and I can feel them around me. I could feel my angel holding me as we walked down the levee. She said, 'Source is within all life, and it is one continuous circle of giving and receiving.' My angel went on to tell me that all humans are energy beings and that I was a light life force of energy much like a rainbow connecting the sky with the earth. Everything is part of the rainbow."

"Maria," Mama said, "you are talking about playing on earth in your giant's eyebrow."

"Now that you mentioned it," I thought out loud, "I guess I am. Funny you should say that, because I can still smell the perfume of the grass and wild flowers. I loved to roll in the grass. It filled me with joy and pushed out the sadness and hurt.

"Oh, Mama, I have only been here in Sacramento for my friend Clifford's

funeral three days, and we have talked about so many things. I appreciate talking to you again. When you transitioned from cancer in the hospital as I held your hand, I never thought I would be able to talk to you and feel your presence again. Here we are visiting.

"I was not equipped to deal with your transition. The family knew your cancer would take your life, but I was not ready. I saw your soul, a small wisp that looked like smoke, leave your body after your last breath came out.

"At that time, I did not know what it was, but the pain was so deep that I ran out of the hospital. I was told I ran for miles before I was stopped. It took me years to work through your death. I had guilt because I was happy you died and your pain was gone, and I was angry with you because as you were dying, all you could say was, 'Take care of your brothers.'

"I wanted you to tell me you loved me, not tell me to take care of my brothers. I was angry at my dad because I thought he mistreated you when you were so sick. I had a hard time forgiving him for that. I did not understand how hard it was for him to lose you. I wanted Dad's approval and love for so many years. After he transitioned, I realized his eyes sparkled when I would show him my artwork and would fuss over him. I was ignorant in not recognizing his love because he did not say, 'I love you, Maria.' He showed me he loved me with his bright eyes.

"I wanted to feel love and hear you two tell me you loved me. I was starving for anyone to love me. I spent most of my life looking for love. Then, when I was soul diving, I realized it was because I did not love myself. I did not know how to love myself.

"That was a long, hard walk, and it took me years to understand what love was. It was so simple once I knew it was built when I did something I felt proud of or did something as simple as making flowers grow. Once I started giving myself a pat on the back for everything I accomplished, I built great love for myself. Then I could hear the compliments, because I earned them from within. That is when I did not need anybody to approve of me. I approved of myself.

"I thought I was finished with soul diving until we started our visits. I still had hidden memories lingering in my being, stored like fat ready to pounce.

"In fairness, the greatest gift you gave me was growing up on the farm where I ran free to play in the woods on the Sacramento River. Animals, trees, and plants were my friends. I would even talk to the fish as my feet splashed through the shallow water, feeling the pebbles and sand between my toes.

"It was always a fun adventure to play outdoors with the whole world as my friend. In fact, the world was my giant. These experiences laid the groundwork in allowing me to recognize my intuition, being psychic, and being part of nature, the stars, the sun, and the universe. I did not know it yet, but I was a part of the whole pure light of life.

"By not loving myself, I created an ego that manifested in the belief that if people didn't like me, they would love my cute eighteen-inch waist and big breasts. I decided that I would be sexy. I would make women look and wish they were me and make men want to have me. I started to use sex in place of love. I was married, but I still wanted love and attention, so 'sexy' would do just fine. My ego was the hardest for me to separate and understand, because the ego is the self in contrast to the world.

"After I was trapped into having to marry Byron, not because I loved him or even that he loved me but because I made a deal, I made a promise under the flag of love and loyalty, and my own emotional turmoil went out of control. I had no place to run.

"There are times when I was my own worst enemy with truth just out of my reach. The hardship of being a wife and mother while being mistreated by my husband caused a lot of pain. I did not know how to describe it or describe what it felt like.

Oh mama. "Long after I got married, the cares and woes of the outside world began crashing in on me. I thought about what would happen if I just ended this life when I heard a familiar voice: 'I am here to help you.' Mama was that you or my spirit guild.

"I heard it, but I did not really hear it. My need to fill my heart and my ego, to struggle for identity and affirmation that I was worthy, blocked my intuition. There was no separation between husband and me. There was no 'me.'

"I would have fantasies that my husband learned of my deepest desires and planned a fabulous getaway surprise. In this fantasy he would talk to me as if I was his biggest fan and speak of how important I was. He would tell me that whatever I wanted he would get it for me, regardless of cost or hardship.

"I continued my life with fantasies and hope, and my ego, along with wishful thinking, became part of my daily life. It was easy to get lost in the thought that maybe tomorrow it would be better and my husband would not beat me or verbally abuse me. I did not know how to cope and became completely separated from my inner voice. Without my inner compass, I became lost in a dark world.

"I thought beating me was the worst he could ever do to me, but it turned out that the worst pain was when he betrayed me with another woman. There is nothing that strips and devastates your soul more than a betrayal. I had a twisted idea that I came to love my husband.

"After that betrayal that was the last day I trusted another person in my life for years to come. Betrayal was more than hurt; it changed the course of my life. I was altered and thrown into a world of hate, anger, and pain that cannot be described. The worst outcome of my pain was that I did not like or trust myself; I blamed myself for not being a better wife. I thought I had given so much. I could not bend my mind around how they could they do that to me in my own home. I was stripped of feeling safe.

"I could deal with being hit and the anger from others, but for me to feel that level of anger was new to me. I became so judgmental that as soon as I would meet people, I would find a lot wrong with them. This stayed with me for too long. When I was altered, not only my emotions changed but my visions changed.

"Now I was full of hate and so was my husband. The fall-out, unfortunately, affected my children, and I did not even see them until I hurt them more than I will ever really know. I now recognize that I was completely blind to their needs because my wounds were so deep I did not know how to stop the emotional bleeding. It felt like ten lifetimes before I could finally look at old memories without stirring up emotions.

"All my affirmations helped me move through what felt like the death of my soul. All steps are meaningful, even if it means going backward. I cried so much to the universe that I experienced synchronicities often, visualizing images of events long before they occurred. Universe answered in a gentle way. "At first they seemed to be random occurrences, but in fact, they were the synchronous manifestations of what I asked the universe to provide. Upon close examination, I could see how I set this into motion. It was my soul gently communicating to

me, telling me to pay attention to the link that my soul has to
the universe and putting together what I set into motion.

"My inner voice told me many things occur on a daily basis
when you ask the universe. Add in meditation with affirmations, and the synchronicities show. With awareness and intent,
anyone can experience wondrous creations.

"Déjà vu is close to synchronicity except that synchronicity
is not an illusion of having already experienced an event, person, place, or thing. You really have traveled there in a dream, or
your spirit was there already. Synchronicity is something you set
in motion when asking the universe to help you by praying or
calling to the universe."

Inherited traits are part of our DNA. We are born with the
knowledge of being connected to the universe and have all of
the answers to all questions within. It is a talent much like being
a singer or a musician. Recognizing this awareness is an illumination of the divine wisdom of knowledge direct from the
source to our heart. I called it a knowing space. It is who we are.

Through the years, my soul's voice was ignored and bat-
tered, but it spoke louder and louder and kept popping up in
dreams and in whispers in my memories.

"Mama," I said, "you see, I collected all parts of me that were
good and bad to put the puzzle together, even sewing together
stitches to piece a whole picture of who Maria Garay was. I
learned to forgive myself and my ex-spouses so I could move
on with my own healing. When I forgave them, they became
my greatest teachers. I also became my own greatest teacher
when I began my class. My intuition brought back the wholeness I had on my giant on the levee of the Sacramento River.

"Well, Mama, what do you think? Did I do good or what?"

"Yes, Maria," she replied. "I am proud of you, and my love

for you is as bright as your rainbow."

I told her, "We have been busy talking and visiting with each other for several days now, and I learned and remembered forgotten events and ideas. The last few pieces I could not understand, even though I forgave you and Dad for not loving me the way I wanted you to.

"I wanted and needed you to show me how much you loved me by helping me be wonderful me. I did not need you to assign me a role of what a woman had to do to endure. I felt you created me so I could be a slave to a man and have children to keep his name living forever. I was not able to completely know my true self until I could understand what I was angry about, why I hurt, why I hated myself, and why I was unable to forgive myself and others. I was unhealthy with many different health problems because, on a cellular level, I felt a deep-seated void of love. Mama, I resented that you did not tell me or show me you loved me. I never heard my dad tell me he loved me either. I looked for love any way I thought I could get it. I used sex, thinking that if I gave sex I would be loved and if did as I was told I would be loved. I thought if I was nice, I would be loved. I looked for love everywhere; I was willing to do anything for that elusive love. Now that you and I have had this conversation about all the resentment and anger I held, I feel grateful and proud you are my mama."

Now I am finished soul diving from my giant's eyebrow. "Mama, I will see you tomorrow and let you know how I will write this conversation about the art of practicing soul diving and then living my life as source."

I had to be completely honest about being good, bad, and ugly, about resentments and anger. That was a tough one, but without that I would still be blind.

CHAPTER 9

Ego

*A*fter talking to my mama for the past week, I sat down with a glass full of iced tea and took a deep breath, feeling relaxed and happy. I was sitting outside in front of my motor home when I realized I had not talked to her about my ego and about the wall I put up around me so nobody could see me.

When I was out of control, I built a big ego to hide behind. I felt self-conscious. I felt I was not pretty because I was Mexican with ugly dresses. Also, I was not able to tell anyone about my abilities. I had a long list of the reasons I did not behave nicely. Yes, at that time I felt sorry for myself, but I came to know that when I judged others, I was judging myself.

When I felt awkward, I would tell myself that the person looking at me was stupid or jealous. I would assume when someone was looking my way she was ragging on me. I was judging myself, because I thought I was an unworthy human being.

My ego would place blame away from me, so that would clear me of any wrongdoing. Then I felt all right for a short time. I knew down deep I was wrong and felt shame and guilt. I kept burying my true self deeper and deeper into Never land so that Maria disappeared.

Assuming I was unworthy and quick to hide, judging became a habit, and expressing an ugly ego that was not me became part of me.

I found that repeating aspects of myself I did not like became part of my identity, but that was not really who I was; it
was just a way to cope. I wanted to be believed. Most of all, I
wanted to believe and love myself. Pain and the need for approval helped create a horrible and judgmental ego.

Making awful, mean remarks sometimes made me feel like I
was better than the person I was judging. I was trapped, because
the faster I ran, the faster I went nowhere. The grove became
deeply ingrained in my mind and unconsciousness. The consequences of that behavior created illness, hate, and self-pity. I had
no friends and felt extremely lonely.

The day I walked into Enthusiasm and Joy Church and
started classes changed my understanding of life, especially my
own life. Meeting people who thought like me was so exhila-
rating. I made many friends and, for the first time, felt normal;
others were just like me. We would compare stories, and all the
members of the class had experiences almost like mine. I finally
felt at ease and sane.

I took another drink of my tea, smiled at the universe, and
said, "Thank you. I am grateful for today." I leaned back on my
chair and put my feet on the chair across from me when I felt a
cool breeze. I said, "Hello, Mama."

"Yes, Mama, I am present and liberated from being just a
human being." I started laughing so loudly that Robert poked
his head out the door and asked if I was all right.

I answered, "Yes, I was just talking to Mama."

"Mama, it is so great to know I am a spiritual being experiencing a human body on earth. I can feel you and other energy beings again. I can even see some energy beings if they want me to. I live a life of amazing wonder and love because I am source. "Tell me, Mama, what did you come to talk to me about?" She answered, "I am here to talk to you about your father. I think you still do not have insight that he did the best he knew how at the time things were going on.

"I know you held your father responsible for my health care when I was so sick. After I passed away you thought your father did not do right raising your younger brother well." Your father did the best he could.

"It is true I was angry with him for a long time. I thought he did not love me because I was a girl. His macho ego was so big and hurtful. All I heard from him was about his sons, the generals. I stayed away, but I did help him with appointments, letters, banks, and the day-to-day stuff.

"Later in his life, when he was older and I lived close to his house, I did visit more with him. I loved him but, I never heard him say he loved or approved of me or even say he believed in me. I did forgive him a long time ago, and yes, I came to realize he did the best he knew how at the moment; he did whatever he had to.

"I remember the past, but I do not let the past use me any longer with emotional pain. I went to visit Dad the week after I went to visit you. I felt sorry that I was not with him at his funeral. I was stuck in Mexico on vacation and could not make it back before my brothers buried him. To this day, I do not talk to them about his funeral. I still think they could have waited. I accepted that I was not supposed to be there at his transition.

"I remember him whole and happy as he showed me his garden and how proud he was. That big ego was no longer in

front of him. So, Mama, do not worry. I am good with Dad and
the man he was.

"I agree that when I was a young kid I did not like his ways,
but I still wanted his approval. I would dance in front of him for
his attention. Remember, Mama, when I used to wash his feet?
I now know the exchange of a smile or a touch speaks of how
much we are loved.

"I loved him, but I did not like the way he treated you,
and his drinking scared me. Growing up, watching him change
when he got drank was seeing two different men. That ego-
driven man who demanded and bossed you around when
drinking became the model for me to accept that all men be-
haved that way. His male friends were just like him, barking
orders and having other women around. They did what they
wanted regardless of who got hurt.

"Their motto was, 'If you do not like it, get out and see who
will take care of you and the children.' For me, that idea held me
imprisoned for years. I had six children, so I thought, 'Where do
I go?' Macho ego is a place of unhappiness driven from fear that
can explode into violent abuse for a whole family.

"What I remember most is when he would get crazy drunk,
we would hide outside in the field, winter or summer, so he
would not hurt us. Mama, somehow your life became my life. I
forgave all memories of hurt for thinking I somehow caused it
all because I was broken. Now I am whole and happy. I am the
observer of life and do not let my memories control my emotions. I am just grateful to be here on earth as a spiritual being
and a human being.

"I just moved back to California from Deming, New Mexico, and left behind the old tradition of that macho behavior
that is alive and well there. I see them judging everybody, not

understanding that they are judging themselves and that anger has consequences. Women do not even have their hair cut without the husband giving them permission. I send out loving energy to help heal that unhappy family abuse because of macho ego. Having a healthy ego is balancing a good sense of being. It is a spiritual being living on earth helping with love and peace."

CHAPTER 10

Affirmations

*I*t was time to head back to New Mexico, so I called the Bear family. The family invited us to meet them at a steak house in south Sacramento to say our farewells.

We came back to the motor home and started preparing to get back on the road. Robert hooked up the car to the back of the motor home and made sure the brakes and lights all worked. We woke up early the next day. I went around the motor home, making sure we were disconnected and nothing was left behind.

It would take us three to four days to make it back to Deming. We planned all our overnight spots and fuel stops and chose the rest areas for our dogs to take a break, stretch their legs, and take care of business. During past trips, it would have taken us longer to travel, but Robert's health did not allow but one day of travel and two or three days of rest.

Almost every day, I meditate. I start by centering, dropping my grounding cord, and running my energy. Once my mind is quiet, if I have problem that I need to resolve, I take care of that first. This routine never changes. In the beginning, I would always do my affirmations to reprogram my old way of thinking and learn a new way of thinking that is for the highest good.

Now I know I am connected to everything and part of source. I will share them with you with the hope that they help you as much as they helped me. Words have a lot of power. The power of ugly words crushed me for a long time, so now I use that power of words for my happiness, you are what you think. My favorite one is as follows:

I Love and Appreciate Myself

`Within me are the power, presence, and completeness of source as I choose to experience the greatness within. I let go of yesterday and any criticism I may have made upon myself. I now release shame, guilt, and any negative thought I may have about myself. I now choose to love myself and accept my good. I am unique and special and realize my strength and limitless power within me.

I would repeat this affirmation for weeks or until I knew, without doubt, and felt each word to be true before I would move on to another affirmation.

I Am

I see clearly that I am whole, perfect, and complete. My awareness is a beacon of light that paves the way for my glorious expression. Happiness and wholeness fill my entire being with the realization that I am perfection.

I Am Grateful

Gratitude is the blessing increasing, amplifying, and attracting power in my experience. Source's good multiplies easily in my life, because I am truly grateful for the divine ideas through me. There is only good. Everything else is a lie. I am thankful for every opportunity in my experience, regardless of its appearance. I am able to see the good in all situations and understand the truth that everything is in divine order. I am thankful that I am claiming and demonstrating divine love in my life. Source is me. I am thankful.

I Love and Appreciate Myself

Within where energy lives are the power, presence, and completeness of source. As I choose to experience the greatness within, I let go of yesterday and any criticism I may have made upon myself. I now release shame, guilt, and any negative thoughts I may have about myself. I now choose to love myself and accept my good. I am unique and special and realize my strength and limitless power within me.

How to Write Your Own Meditations

Title/Purpose:
This treatment is to cause me to _____ and experience/have and be in perfect fulfillment with regard to _____.

Decree: I Am Fulfillment
Recognition:
Spirit is infinite energy, perfect love, absolute good, awareness, and fulfillment. Thank you.

Elimination:
I call upon myself (*I am*) to consume and dissolve all negative thought forms. Lift, bless, and heal all seeming negation. I

call upon forgiveness to dissolve all cause, effect, memory, and record of any seeming error that touches my life stream. I cut all psychic ties between myself and all people, situations, and circumstances that are not for my highest good. Thank you.

Realization:

I realize, know, and accept that source is I am, as above so below. I am absolute good and perfect love, particularly with regard to the immediate manifestation of perfect fulfillment in

_____.

Gratitude:

I am grateful and filled with joy that I now have perfect fulfillment. Thank you.

Release:

I release this meditation to universe for perfect right action. Thank you.

Always give thanks to source for helping you achieve your highest self.

Divine Gift

Today I consciously share in the gift of life. I open my whole thought and my divine being to the divine influx. I empty myself of everything that denies the good I desire. I establish my mind in positive expectancy, knowing that all the good there is belongs to anyone who will take it. I receive the divine gift right now. I enter right now into my spiritual inheritance. Today I am richly blessed of the gift of life that flows through me, through all avenues. I consciously choose to move through my fears by swinging out into the unknown and enjoying the experiences that trust in the universe reveals.

It took me years to work through all my abuse, fears, resentment, hurt, emotional tribulation, loneliness, and not knowing who Maria was.

The day I walked into the Church of Enthusiasm and Joy I met and discovered me. I did all the work step by step. Learning about being a spiritual being first was a springboard to knowing I am source and my true self.

Today I am a healer, psychic medium, minister of metaphysical science, Reiki master/teacher, shaman, and spiritual coach. My favorite subject to teach is to help open psychic abilities in everyone.

I am a teacher of Ernest Holmes teachings and metaphysical knowledge.